D1189687

KEPT IN THE DARK

KEPT IN THE DARK

J. RONALD M. YORK

Kept in the Dark
J. Ronald M. York
p. cm.

ISBN 978-0-9982734-2-6

This book is printed on acid-free paper.

First Edition

visit www.JRonaldMYork.com

For Jade,

who along with
Erin, Jeremy, Carol, Bing, Stacy,
Al, Bradley & Rodger
listened without prejudice and
supported without questioning.

And to the loving memories
that I still hold dear of my parents.

FOREWORD

You are about to meet some people that I have known for decades. Allow me a few moments to tell you about them.

I have known Ron York, as well as his parents Joyce and Bob, for as long as I have memories. Our families met at First Baptist Church in downtown Nashville long ago, and our parents became part of an informal group that often gathered at various homes following Sunday evening services. This was all the rage at the time. At first, like most children, I identified Joyce and Bob as "Ron's parents." But these two special people made themselves personally known to those of us in our group, and to many, many, more. They became some of our first "adult friends" because they treated us with love and respect.

As I look back, the public personas of Joyce and Bob could not have been more different. Joyce was the sweetest mother and lady anyone could have known. She was always kind beyond description to the younger folks and all children, was beautiful, and was the consummate lady in a time when "ladyhood" was stressed. Bob always played a little gruff. I say "played" because that is exactly what it was, a facade. Inside he was one of the sweetest, most caring men one might know. If you had a need, he was there with an answer. If you needed some gentle, or not so gentle, persuasion to do the right thing, Bob was there. He was also a respected businessman in the larger community of Nashville.

Even though Joyce and Bob were from the (then) distant land of Florida, Miami even (!) they fit right in with the Southern gentility of the time. Everything Joyce did was just right. Having people over, feeding them, being the perfect hostess, all of that and more was Joyce York. Her death at a fairly early age was tragic, but Joyce handled her rapidly advancing cancer with aplomb, with a sweet spirit, and with her beauty and loving nature intact until the end.

When Bob died it came as a shock to all. Unlike Joyce, Bob left this life unexpectedly, when he had an automobile accident after an apparent heart attack. By the time Ron got to see him, all he could do was give permission for life support to be removed and bid his father farewell. One of the great honors of my life as a pastor and friend of Ron's was to be asked to say some things in memory of Bob at his funeral. I don't remember exactly what I said, but I was moved almost to tears when Bob's sister came up to me after the funeral and said, "You got it right. You knew who Bob was."

Ron is one of my favorite people in all the world. He is simply Ron, sweet as can be, slightly tart, OK, maybe a little more than "slightly" when it is called for, a wonderful artist, proud gallery owner and astute businessman. Ron wears so many hats with so many organizations around town that I honestly don't see how he does it all. His commitment to the arts and community relations is simply amazing. I am proud to call him my friend, and profoundly glad that his voice speaks into my life regularly. Ron had a very close relationship with my mother, who is now with her Lord and her friend Joyce York. Ron and I joke that he was the son my mother wished she'd had! I love dropping by the gallery occasionally and just spending a little time with Ron. It is always great conversation and fun, punctuated with wonderful hugs with my friend and brother.

The story you are about to read is one in which you will meet each of these three people: Joyce, Bob, and Ron York. The story unfolds in a much different place from that in which I knew this family; a different place geographically, a different place emotionally, and a different place culturally.

The story unfolds in a surprising way, and is unlike any you have read before. All families have their individual stories, stories of all facets of the family's life. These stories are passed down by word of mouth, and they inform where we came from, where we are, where our children are, and what our history is, all in the arc of the stories. When we know these stories, it helps to determine the trajectory on which we were launched. These stories do not determine our end results nor who we are, but they are our launch pad.

The great Southern writer Wendell Berry is said to ask three questions of everyone he meets: "Where are you from?" "Who are your people?" "What do you grow?" These questions form the basis of the oral tradition of all of our families, what we "know" about our families, both nuclear, and from generations past.

What happens when one of those stories is missing or hidden? An important story. A story that is in some ways crucial to the development of a family and its story arc?

What happens when one member of that family finds out about the hidden story decades after it happened? What memories, what treasured recollections, what pieces of the family puzzle are changed? How does that affect the individual who discovered it?

As you read this story, lovingly and honestly told, you will begin to see how one man worked through what a missing story meant to him. You will almost inevitably be forced to ask yourself about your own family, not necessarily in a questioning manner, but in one that might make you want to know more about your family story arc and where it has brought you.

I highly recommend this book to you. Read it with a mind ready to tackle sudden turns and twists, and let it push you back toward your own family and learning more about who they are, and who you are.

— Bing Davis

Bob & Joyce York, November 29, 1946

PROLOGUE

Secrets. We all have them, and we all hope they will never be revealed. My parents, relatives and a handful of close friends took our family secret to their graves. And yet, my parents held on to a box of incriminating evidence, through five moves in three different cities, to be left for me to find long after everyone was gone.

You may already be questioning my motives. Am I trying to embarrass my parents? Is this some sort of payback for an injustice I felt they did to me? Or am I trying to profit from their mistake? Actually, it is none of these. I considered never saying a word. However, my hope in sharing this would be that it might help someone in a similar situation.

May I ask that, before you turn the page and begin this journey with me, you keep an open mind and heart? This is a true story. The people involved are real, as is the heartache, pain, struggles, frustrations, and love. It is easy to see the crime and immediately judge. By no means am I suggesting that you shouldn't feel this emotion. I am not condoning the actions committed. You may wish me to condemn, but this tale is not just black or white. Please know that I am not withholding facts or trying to cover up anything. I want you, the reader, to know everything that I know.

I feel I was blessed with loving and supportive parents. I know that they could have easily destroyed this evidence from the past and I would never have known, or even suspected, that there was anything amiss. By saving it, I think they wanted me to have this knowledge, to process it, and to decide where and how it fits into my life. I ask the same from you. Please consider everything involved before passing judgement. There is no right or wrong way for you to feel once you've read my story.

KEPT IN THE DARK

ONE.

" Baby, when all of this is over, we ought to really
be able to write a love story, because I don't
believe anyone could love deeper
or greater than we do."
Joyce York, December 12, 1955

It was nothing more than a box of love letters, tossed into a discarded liquor box, that I found on that beautiful summer day. The box was tucked inside a wooden trunk painted Army green with the Boy Scout emblem, painted in black, on top. Together they were left in the detached storage shed behind our family home.

I, with help from a few friends, was sorting through 40 years of accumulation, preparing for an estate sale, now that my father had passed away. I was alone in the shed when I opened the box. The warm sun on that July day made the different smells inside seem more pronounced. Grass clippings left on the lawn equipment, with a hint of gasoline from the can for the mower, mixed with the aroma of the shed's raw wood construction, and the mustiness wafting up as I opened the trunk and the cardboard box of letters. As a curious child, I had opened the same box many years before, while my mother was still alive, after I discovered it while rummaging through her closet. The letters were bundled in stacks, and held together by rubber bands. Nothing at that time enticed me to dig deeper into the box. However, rediscovering the box, which had clearly been moved to this new hiding place, I found the contents had shifted. The letters, no longer in neatly bundled stacks, looked as if they had been read and tossed back into the box. I realized in that brief moment that not all of the letters were addressed or postmarked the same. And on top was a yellowed newspaper clipping. After one glance, I quickly closed the box and placed it in my car before anyone helping me had a chance to ask about what I had found.

I stored the box in my garage for several years. Now that I have finally chosen to come face to face with its contents, I find that I am left frustrated. No, not just frustrated. I am also mad, hurt, and a little bit confused. I have had a good life, and have wonderful childhood memories. I feel thankful and blessed. However, at an age when I should be applying for Social Security, I find myself on a journey of discovery, as I unlock painful secrets, and piece together a life I never knew existed, all because of a box of letters. I have been shown a crack in my family's facade.

How could I not be angry with my parents, especially my father, for keeping this secret from me? And yet a box of letters, exchanged between my parents more than 60 years ago, was left for me to discover. I don't believe that it was forgotten, or overlooked. I think it was intentional. But more than anything, I am sad, because it was the most difficult challenge my family ever went through, and I have no memory of it at all.

In my defense, the events took place when I was two years old, on the cusp of turning three. I realize now that dozens of family members and close friends have always known the story, actually lived through it with my parents, and yet never let a word slip out in front of me. People who were a part of my life growing up obviously respected my parents to the point of keeping this secret buried in the past.

The anger I feel is directed more at myself than my parents. If I had read the letters when I found them nearly 16 years ago, there would have been several family members and friends who lived through this difficult time still alive and able to share with me firsthand information. But now, all of these years later, almost everyone is gone.

For months now, I have been traveling down dead end roads and walking through doors that lead nowhere, trying to assemble this tale. I have searched for family friends mentioned in the letters only to find that they are gone. I have even tried to locate their children, but they too have passed away. My father's youngest half-sister shared with me what she knew, as did as my uncle who had been married to mother's youngest sister. Just bits and pieces from what remaining family I have left.

I reached out to the court systems and the public library for legal documents and newspaper articles. I even spoke with a psychic who, before I said a word, saw the confusion I've been going through over several months, my range of emotions and my need to write it all down. I was told my discovery happened when it was supposed to and my story will be of help to others. But more importantly, I was told that it was not my fault.

As I think back now, the only hint that something was amiss was the total lack of communication between our family and that of my mother's older sister, Betty, her husband Buddy, and sons Robert and Brian. I have an old photo from 1954 of my cousins and me. Brian and I would have been two years old and Robert would have been 13 years old – an age that, in light of what I've found, is very significant. This photo lets me see that at one time our families might have been close, but by the next year, that was over.

We lived in Miami, Florida, my birthplace, as well as my mother's home and birthplace. Her sweet mother, my proper and demure grandmother, was originally from Nashville, Michigan, and in December of 1920, hitchhiked with a girlfriend to Miami. They were arrested in Atlanta for wearing men's clothing. However, the case was dismissed when a policewoman told the court: "I think these two girls are more decently dressed than lots of the little girls who parade Peachtree and Whitehall in a handful of clothing."

I don't believe that anyone meeting my grandmother would have suspected that she could have been this adventurous or daring. But then, we are not always what we appear to be. She had been a small town schoolteacher, who found a friend that shared a love for David Grayson's *"The Friendly Road"* and the "natural tendency to wanderlust," according to a newspaper article. They traveled to Toledo, Cincinnati, and on through to Lexington, and then Louisville, Kentucky. They are quoted as saying, "Country people in Kentucky had been taking us in for the night and giving us our breakfast." They even visited Mammoth Cave.

In Shelbyville, Tennessee, a Methodist preacher gave them Sunday dinner at his home and their first taste of fried pie. They were stopped in Cowan, Tennessee, by some railroad men, because two girls had escaped from the Tennessee Girls' Industrial School and they thought they might have been the escapees. After they explained their situation, the men took up a collection to put them on a train, saying it was too dangerous for them to walk through the mountains. They arrived in Chattanooga and were arrested because of their apparel. The charges were dismissed. The matron had them put on skirts over their army pants so they would be able to gain admission to the Y.W.C.A.

In Ringgold, Georgia, a federal prohibition officer *(Prohibition was enforced from 1920 to 1933)* gave them a letter addressed to "all chivalrous Georgia men and good Georgia women" that helped them establish themselves in the different towns they visited. After Atlanta, they passed through Macon, and Jacksonville, before arriving in Miami.

I know of this, not because my grandmother ever told me the story, but because after she passed away, I found, hidden deep in her cedar chest, a front page clipping, with photos, from Atlanta's *Sunday American* newspaper dated December 19, 1920. In Miami, she found love, married, and had four daughters.

This kind of family secret is endearing. However, many years later, in another trunk, in another city, I uncovered a family secret that is dark, and unsettling, and which left me stunned.

My father was born in Tampa, Florida but his family moved to Miami when he was a teenager. He would tell the story that, as a senior high school student, he had to step in and direct the high school chorus for the remainder of the school year after his teacher committed suicide. Ten years later, at age 28, his talent, ability, and love of music offered him the opportunity to lead the music for Christian evangelist Billy Graham when he brought his crusades to Miami in 1949. Thirty years later, my mother served on the committee to bring The Billy Graham Crusades to Nashville, Tennessee, which had become our home after the events of 1955-56. I remember standing with my father in 1979, when he asked Rev. Graham if he remembered a young guy leading the music for him in Miami many years ago. With a smile, Graham replied, "The fellow I remember was much thinner."

As a student directing the chorus in high school, my dad told a pretty young girl, the 12-year-old Joyce Broadway, five years his junior, that he was going to marry her one day. She would say he was arrogant, but everyone knew she was smitten. Eight years later, on November 29, 1946, they were married at Central Baptist Church in downtown Miami.

Dr. C. Roy Angell, aka "Preacher," officiated and my grandfather, James York, served as best man. My mother's older sister, Betty, was matron of honor, and her son Robert was listed as page. My mother's younger sister, June, served as maid of honor. Some of my dad's groomsmen included Earl Culbreth and Cecil Carroll, with whom he worked at Independent Life and Accident Company. Cecil's daughter, Barbara, was the flower girl, and my dad's much younger cousin from Alabama, George Culver, was ring bearer.

Ed Kaplan, also with Independent Life and who, in spite of his Jewish faith, would dress up and play Santa Claus each Christmas, was another groomsman. Earl Culbreth, in later years, would share the story of how Kap's Santa suit came to be. The origin goes back to World War II when Earl and his fellow soldiers, crossed the Rhine River traveling through Dusseldorf and Cologne. He said: "At that time they had a lot of banner-like flags hanging out the doors and the two story buildings and all, with the Nazi symbol on it and you know red and white and black are the German's colors." He went on to say that they were called flags but they were actually more like a banner and he was able to acquire one and send it back home. Once he returned home, he showed it to Kap, "and him being a Jew and hating the Germans more so maybe than what we did, he wanted it so bad." Earl gave the banner to Kap, and he took it to a seamstress and had a Santa suit made. Earl went on to say Kap played Santa for 10 years or more and would laugh saying "here's a Jew, American Jew, you know, wearing a German outfit playing Santa Claus." My family used a photo of Kap, in that Santa suit holding me, for our Christmas card.

Another groomsman standing at the end of the back row in the wedding photograph was Guy Cutulo, the assistant Scoutmaster of Troop One at Central Baptist Church where my father served as Scoutmaster. It is evident, as a friend for many years, he was deeply intertwined in their lives. However, until now, he had never been a part of mine.

Cousins Brian & Robert Morrison with Ron York

Santa Ed "Kap" Kaplan with Ron York

*Hitchhikers Catherine Hilliard &
Mary Walker (Broadway)*

Mother and Daughter

TWO.

My mother loved Miami. Her home, her friends, her family, her church and her life were there. And yet, somehow, we ended up in Tennessee by the time I was four.

My childhood memories begin in Tennessee… our home, my room, my friends, my school, and at age seven my first time to be sexually molested. I never told my parents. Not about the first time, when it happened at church, nor the times that followed. I think it was because I didn't want them to be disappointed in me. Or that maybe I thought I would be in trouble for doing something wrong. It seems that I, too, was good at keeping secrets. I also never told them of that Boy Scout overnight camp-out, when I was a young teen, and about the sexual encounter that was mutual with a boy my own age. I think it was then that I realized I had a choice.

I was raised in a loving home. We were not wealthy, but I don't recall ever being in need. My father worked for Independent Life and Accident Insurance Company. Their home office was in Jacksonville, Florida and he was a salesman in the Miami office. Eventually, he was transferred to Nashville, Tennessee to open a district office there. The company first expanded with an office in Chattanooga, where we lived for nine months before moving to Nashville. I don't remember much from that time other than my parents talking about what an unpleasant experience it turned out to be. Chattanooga in the 1950s was a far cry from the exciting, bustling city of Miami. And then there was the cold and the snow. It was a novelty at first, but something my mother never fully embraced. I can remember her telling me that if I buried her in the cold, hard Tennessee ground, that she would come back and haunt me. Don't think that didn't cross my mind on May 11, 1985 when we buried her, at age 58, in Tennessee soil.

In 1956, my mother drove from Miami to Chattanooga in a used 1952 green Cadillac with me, our dog "Little Girl," and a bird. As an adult, I got to hear my mother tell the story of that trip. She said that she was crying and speeding as she crossed the Florida state line. Then, the police pulled her over, and as she rolled down the window, the dog jumped out and I started crying. The policeman chased our dog, caught her and put her back in the car. In tears, my mother began explaining about leaving her home and with that, the policeman said, "Lady, you have problems enough. I'm not going to give you a ticket. Just drive on." She kept to herself the real reason we were leaving Miami for Tennessee.

After our time in Chattanooga, we moved to Nashville and rented a small home near the airport, as construction was being finished on our new home on the west side of town. We moved in just in time for me to start elementary school at age five. The school was within walking distance. My closest friends consisted of three neighbor girls: one to the left of our home, one to the right, and one across the street. I was always more comfortable around girls, because I was often bullied by boys.

My mother eventually went to work for the Christian Life Commission of the Southern Baptist Convention, giving me a couple of hours after school alone until one or both of my parents came home. My father was the district manager for the Nashville office of Independent Life and Accident Insurance company, but eventually advanced to a position that involved travel. He would be gone during the week but home on weekends. This lasted only a couple of years and I don't recall any conflict. I was perfectly content with just my mom. At night we would fix dinner and put up a card table in front of the TV to eat. *(Something that I now know had been our routine those last few months in Miami.)*

Eventually the travel got old and my dad went back to his original position with the company and stayed in town. My mother found another job with better pay. I graduated high school and began my freshman year at a local school, Belmont College, *(now University)*. I lived on campus in a dorm, and felt freedom like I had never known. I studied voice and piano and made life-long friends.

During my sophomore year, my dad made the decision to leave Independent Life and work for a local insurance agency while he pursued a career in financial planning. It takes time to build a business and, although I was in college, they could, fortunately, still count on my mother's income. Then the unthinkable happened — the company my mother worked for closed. I can only imagine the financial burden. Unfortunately, I remember too well the spoiled, selfish, only child in me coming out as I was forced to move out of the dorm and back home for my junior year. However, by my senior year, with two part-time jobs *(Church music director and music store sales help)*, I moved into an off-campus apartment with a friend.

The apartment was a dump across the street from Belmont's campus. My roommate, John, was a fellow student whom I would often refer to as a chameleon. He could adapt by becoming whatever he felt he needed to be. He was basically straight, but had no problem acting gay if it suited him or his cause. He was educated and talented, but had inner demons that plagued him until the end. I think back now and realize that I had a love/hate relationship with him. Now, I am left with a feeling of regret for losing touch with him before it was too late.

John was friends with another student, Larry, who was definitely gay, and who also became a friend of mine, and eventually our roommate, when the three of us moved into a larger apartment. Our newest addition to our dysfunctional family turned out to be the nephew of friends of my parents from our days in Miami. And now, decades later, I find a card of encouragement his aunt sent to my parents during the time of their ordeal in 1955-56. All through this journey of discovery, I have been amazed by the volume of unexpected things that are connected.

My father's business flourished, allowing my mother the choice of not returning to work. A friend invited her to a Christian Women's Club luncheon, which she enjoyed and she began going monthly, becoming more and more involved. She started by serving on the decorations committee and eventually became president of the club. From there my mother moved into a position of overseeing the area club chapters.

I had never known my mom as a public speaker but treasure the time I had the chance to listen to her speak, telling her story, motivating and touching the lives of those women in attendance. At one club luncheon, meeting in a neighboring town's Holiday Inn, the program consisted of my mother speaking and I was to sing a solo. I still laugh when I think of how she began her talk with a combination of both of my parents' senses of humor. She started by sitting a shoebox on the podium and saying she had shared with my father how nervous she was to speak in front of so many. Then, she said he gave her this box and told her that when she gets nervous, to open it, place it to her ear, and relax. She opened the box and pulled out a phone, putting the receiver to her ear, and began talking. As the room broke out in laughter, she began her tale of where she came from and how the Lord brought her to this point. However, none of the ladies, or even I, got to hear about those months in 1955 that changed her life.

My dad opened his own insurance agency to go along with his successful financial planning business. My parents were finally at a point where they could relax and enjoy their life together. They traveled often, with friends, here and abroad. They taught a Sunday School class for young married couples at church and served on committees and boards. At one point, my dad was a Trustee for the Southern Baptist Sunday School Board, now LifeWay Christian Resources, the publishing arm of the Southern Baptist Convention.

In 1978, my father had the winning bid on a small midtown office building being auctioned. He moved his businesses into half of the first floor and I renovated the second floor into my living quarters. The following year, my mother and I opened the Mistletoe Shop, "where it's Christmas year 'round," in the other half of the first floor. To do this, I had to agree to work part-time in my dad's insurance agency, which I did for a while. Finally, he was convinced that it was not for me. He reluctantly agreed I could devote all of my time to the retail shop. It was such a blessing to work with my mother, sharing our love of Christmas, for the first five years.

Joyce with Ron, Chattanooga, 1956

Christian Women's Club luncheon

Ron holding Puddin', Mistletoe Shop, Nashville, 1981

Joyce, Mistletoe Shop, Nashville, 1981

THREE.

At the age of 57, my mother was diagnosed with renal cell cancer. It appeared as a small lump on her waist, in what the doctors described as just a fatty tumor and nothing to be alarmed about. But then, they did a biopsy. Another lump soon appeared on her neck and then one on her shoulder, causing her arm to break. This couldn't be happening. She was too young.

If someone had asked me a year earlier how I thought my mother would react in such a situation, my answer would have been totally different than what actually happened. My mother was beautiful inside and out. She was not vain but she was always "put together," fashionable and stylish. With a knot on her neck and her arm in a sling, I would have predicted that my mother would find excuses to stay home, almost becoming reclusive. However, it was just the opposite. She got up, dressed, threw a scarf around her neck and continued living. She was an inspiration to everyone. I kept asking the Lord why He would take her now, when she was doing so much good in His name.

My dad, always the strong one, was barely holding up. He couldn't talk with me about it and held back information trying to protect me. This led to me having to talk directly with her doctors, who were still somewhat guarded.

When she came to terms with the fact that there was no hope of recovery, there were two things she wanted to do. First, was to go with me to the Atlanta market, one last time, to buy for our Christmas store. The other was to go on a trip with my dad.

I drove us to the January market in Atlanta, as I had so many times before. Although thin, she was still so beautiful. The chemo had not worked and had made her weaker. However, one small blessing was she had not lost her hair with the treatment.

Many of the showrooms we visited were ones we had worked with through the years. Everyone was aware of our situation and they were all so attentive. A chair would be brought out for her to sit in, and we all worked at her pace.

On that Sunday morning in January, 1985, we were getting dressed in our motel room. I had the TV on and the televangelist, Rev. Ernest Angley, was laying his hands on people and yelling "heal." Normally I might have made fun of him, but in desperation and with tears streaming down my face, I turned to my mother and said, "I will put you in the car right now and drive you there if you want to go and let him lay his hands on you." She looked at me with so much compassion and love, reminding me that the Lord's hands were already on her and we must not question but accept his will. I held her for a long time and once the tears stopped flowing, we dressed and went to the gift market for our last time together.

My dad had a business trip scheduled for late February in Florida. My mother, getting weaker every day, was determined to go. My dad tried to make it as normal as possible, but later regretted not upgrading to first class, and not having a wheelchair waiting for her. By the time she got home, she could no longer hide the pain.

For several years, I had a part-time music director's job at Carroll Street Chapel. It was a small mission of our home church, First Baptist. Each Mother's Day, I would sing a special song dedicated to my mother, and my parents would attend the service. Her favorite song for me to sing was *"He Touched Me."* It is a lovely song and the "He" of course, is referring to our Lord, Jesus Christ. But in light of everything I now know, the title has a completely different meaning to me. The song was written in 1963 by the legendary, William J. Gaither. Now, all of these years later, as I read the lyrics from the first verse, I think I understand fully why this song resonated so much with my mother.

"Shackled by a heavy burden, 'neath, a load of guilt and shame:
Then the hand of Jesus touched me, and now I am no longer the same."

"Heavy burden," check. *"Guilt,"* check. *"Shame,"* check.

At the time of my mother's illness, I was back at First Baptist singing in the choir. I had asked our Minister of Music if I could sing the solo on Mother's Day for my mother. He agreed, but knew that it would be a very emotional thing for me to do. A few weeks before Mother's Day, he called me to say the soloist for the upcoming Sunday had to cancel and he wondered if I'd like to go ahead and sing now, not waiting for Mother's Day. My mother was clearly getting weaker with each day, so I agreed to move up the date.

That glorious Sunday morning, I approached the podium and looked up at the smiling face of my mother seated next to my father in the balcony. With the sun illuminating the stained glass windows, the pianist began to play and I sang her favorite song. When I finished, the congregation erupted in applause. The applause was not for me. No, their applause was a way of showing their love and support for my mother and our family. That turned out to be the last Sunday my mother was strong enough to attend a church service.

A few weeks later, on the weekend of Mother's Day, my precious mom passed away. At her funeral service, the first floor of the church sanctuary was filled to capacity. So many flowers were sent that my dad and I requested an arrangement be placed in each of the Sunday School classrooms for the next morning's worship.

FOUR.

I was now left with my father. We had always had my sweet mother as a buffer. I often felt that I was somewhat of a disappointment to him, although I was told by others how proud he was of me. There was never a question that he loved me, but our relationship did not have the closeness that I felt with my mother.

My dad decided to move his offices, one block away, into his recently purchased building that his former employer, Independent Life, had rented for many years. This allowed the Mistletoe Shop to expand into the other half of the first floor and stay in our present location.

It wasn't long before my father, who visited the store often, came in and pointed out what he believed had not been done and needed to be done. Of course, this set me off and ended with him storming out. I went straight back into the office and picked up the phone to call my mother as I had always done. I would tell her what had happened and she would ask me to wait until she heard his side of the story and then she would help us work it out. As the phone began to ring, it started to sink in that she was no longer there to answer. I put the receiver back in place, took a deep breath, picked it up again and called my dad. When he answered, I said, "You know we now have to work this out ourselves." He confessed that he had just had the same thought.

I can't tell you that there was an immediate change, but we did reach a point of trying not to push each other's buttons, nor to overreact when we occasionally did.

My dad struggled for more than a year with her loss. He drank more than he should have and he exhausted friends with his depressed mood, his stories, and tears. I had calls from his friends expressing concern. There were times that I would call to check on him at night and realize, from slurred words, that he had had too much to drink. When I would mention the call to him the next day, he would have no recollection of our conversation.

I am happy to say that he eventually turned himself around. He became so active at church that he was there practically every time the doors opened. In fact, as chair of the church's grounds committee, he even had his own key. He was always trying to support and help those in need.

Our relationship grew stronger. With my mother gone, my dad and I made the decision to close the Mistletoe Shop in its twelfth year. I focused on my interior design business, which lead me to open my first art gallery. Dad was supportive, and even though there were times he questioned my decisions, he did not become bullheaded and argumentative as he had in the past.

My design business flourished and gave me many opportunities to travel. I was blessed with several clients having second homes in Florida which they would offer to me as a vacation getaway. There were times when I would invite Dad to join me. Although he often would only stay a day or two, he would at least take me up on the offer.

He became accepting of my friends and no longer questioned my being gay. I believe the first time I ever saw him cry, long before my mother became ill, was when an "ex" of mine, from a relationship that had gone sour, called him to "out" me. My mother and I had already discussed my sexuality. Although I can't imagine him being surprised by the news, I think actually hearing it said out loud made it become real. In light of what I now know, I can't help but wonder if his emotional reaction came from guilt in thinking his actions might have been the cause of my sexual orientation. Or now, knowing what my mother lived through those last months in Miami, he may have wondered if she blamed him. Eventually he sold his insurance agency and office building and moved his financial planning business home. He continued to work hard and stayed active in church.

One tradition my parents kept alive, until the very end, was for me to always have an Easter basket. This turned into more of a challenge as I became older, and was sometimes was not in town on Easter Sunday. They often would enlist the help of friends to pull it off. Another tradition that started, once we opened the Christmas Shop, was to give me the Royal Copenhagen annual plate each Christmas.

On Easter morning 2000, I opened my car door to find my dad had been by that morning and had left my Easter basket on the front seat. The contents of my baskets varied over the years. Candy was now narrowed down to my favorite, Peanut M&Ms. He would still take the time to dye hard-boiled eggs for me but now included a small jar of mayonnaise and one of pickle relish, so that I could turn them into egg salad. However, this year, along with the usual goodies, was the 2000 Christmas plate. When I met him for lunch after church, I thanked him but admitted being surprised by the gift of the plate and the fact that he did not wait until Christmas. He said he didn't see the need in waiting. He wanted me to have it now. At that time, neither of us knew that we had already spent our last Christmas together.

That June, I planned a getaway to Marco Island, Florida, staying at the beautiful waterfront condominium of one of my design clients, who was also a dear friend. She had been close to my mother and, after my mother passed away, became like a second mother to me. I could easily be myself around her and realized my mother had shared some confidences with her. There was absolutely no judgement, only love.

I invited my dad to join me in Marco Island. He agreed and surprisingly stayed for longer than the usual two days. The trip fell over Father's Day and I asked him what he would like to do to celebrate. He suggested we drive to Miami for the day and so we got in the car and headed south. Once we were there, we rode around looking at the places that had been a part of my mother's and his life there. He told me stories that I had heard over and over through the years, and a few that I had not.

I wanted to drive by my grandmother's home. I knew it had been torn down after we sold it, but still, I needed to go by there. Neighboring homes stood in various stages of neglect on this downtown street but, in my mind, I could still see that two-story frame bungalow with the wicker rockers and porch swing where we would sit and drink Pepsi trying to stay cool at night. It was the home where my mother and her three sisters were raised. For me, it was a magical place full of wonderful memories.

But now, I realized that, for my mother and my grandmother, within those walls, a family became divided, and my father was to blame.

Broadway Family Home, Miami

Bob after purchasing former employer's office building

THE MIAMI HERALD
Friday, November 18, 1955

Page 28C

Psychiatric Test Ordered for Accused Molester

Immediate psychiatric examinations were ordered in Criminal court Thursday for Robert L. York, 34, former Miami insurance salesman, who admitted to committing lewd acts with a school boy.

York, who pleaded guilty Nov. 3 and was leaving Florida under a suspension of sentence when re-arrested, went back before Judge Ben C. Willard on a new complaint, filed by the boy's father.

"This man has pleaded guilty," the judge said Thursday. "Have him placed in (county) jail and get two psychiatrists to check him on the question of whether or not he is a 'criminal sexual psychopath' (as defined in a new Florida law).

"When they are ready, have them report to me their finding without recommendations and we'll see if this case should be handled in the Circuit court (as a sexual psychopath) or in this court (on the criminal offense).

"From now on, we'll handle all these (sex) cases this way no matter who they are or who represents them," the court declared.

York, married and a father, was accused of molesting a 13-year-old member of his church Boy Scout troop last year.

Also charged with three offenses involving boys of the same troop, Guy Cutulo, 38, 1348 NW Seventh St., suspended Citrus Grove physical education instructor, Thursday pleaded innocent and demanded a jury trial in Judge Willard's court, set for Dec. 5-7.

Cutulo is free under $3,000 bond.

Scoutmaster Bob York

Assistant Scoutmaster Guy Cutulo

FIVE.

On July 10th, 2000, one month after our Father's Day trip, my dad was headed to help one of his elderly clients move to an apartment in assisted living. Two friends were there to help him pack, and I was to come later to arrange furniture and hang pictures.

My father was not just punctual, but often early, a trait that I seemed to have inherited. His friends called me when he was 30 minutes late, wondering if I knew where he might be. I began calling his cell phone, which would repeatedly go to voicemail. Something was wrong. Something had to be wrong, as my dad was never late.

I kept calling, and then finally someone answered. I knew it wasn't him, and asked if this was even his phone. The man on the other end said yes, and asked if I was his son. I was talking to a policeman. My dad had been in a single car accident, hitting a tree and flipping the car. I was told he had been rushed to Vanderbilt Hospital, a perfectly good hospital, but I knew my dad preferred Baptist Hospital. That was what was going through my mind as I rushed to see him: I had to move him to Baptist Hospital. Funny, the strange things you remember.

I called one of my dearest friends who met me at the hospital. We were led into a private waiting room the size of a walk-in closet. A doctor came in and explained to us that my dad's condition was critical and that he was being kept alive by machines. They thought he had had a heart attack, which caused the wreck, but it was the internal injuries from not wearing a seatbelt that were the most serious. They advised me that there was nothing to be done except to turn off the machines.

I was sitting there, stunned and in shock, in a hospital that my dad did not like, while this total stranger gave me the heartbreaking news. By then, family and friends were gathering in the larger waiting area. All I could do was put my trust in God that this was the right choice. My very independent father would have never wanted to be dependent on anyone or anything. That much I knew for sure.

I nodded and the doctor took me back to my father's bed. It seemed like machines were everywhere making noise. How could he be sleeping? He was always such a light sleeper. The doctor turned off the machines and the noise stopped. I put my hand on his and sat with him until he took his last breath. It had been just a few hours since I heard the policeman say there had been an accident. And now, I was walking out of the hospital with a small plastic bag of his personal items, feeling more alone than I could have possibly imagined.

There was a blur of activity for days, but what I remember most was standing for hours at the funeral home as people from our past and present shook my hand and told me stories of how my father had helped them and what he meant to them. I never knew about all of the times that he had counseled, put in a good word, co-signed, given money, given a job, or in some other way was there in someone's darkest hour and so much more. I was overwhelmed by the outpouring of love from all of the lives he had touched.

As I said from the beginning, I was blessed with loving parents. They were generous, thoughtful, and devoted to each other. My father never remarried after my mother died. He had barely even dated in the 15 years since my mother had passed away. He had found the love of his life. I think that I knew that long before I read the letters that they exchanged over the two months they were apart in 1955. After my dad passed away, I was faced with the daunting job of selling his business, and going through four decades of accumulation, to prepare our family home for sale. I don't know where the energy came from, but with the help of friends, it was accomplished in record time.

In the storage shed, filled with tools and lawn equipment, I found the box of letters. Some are from my father addressed to my mother at their Miami home address. The others are from her, addressed to my father in care of the Miami-Dade County Jail 21N, with the word "censored" stamped on the envelope.

I researched and found out that the Miami-Dade County courthouse was the tallest building in all of Florida when it was built in 1928. In 1955-56, when these letters were written, the top nine floors of the 28-story building housed the jail. My father was on the 21st floor with windows looking down on one of Miami's main thoroughfares, Flagler Street.

I have learned that my father was arrested for the original crime in 1954, to which he pleaded guilty, and was given a suspended sentence at trial on November 1,1955, under the conditions that he and his family leave the state of Florida. However, two days later, as he stopped in Jacksonville on his way to Charleston, South Carolina, he was rearrested and returned to Miami. Another charge had surfaced, resulting in him spending eight weeks in jail awaiting trial.

The letters are from this eight week period, as he was brought to trial for a second time. I do not know all of the particulars of the original trial or everything my parents went through at that time. However, I do know about the charge from reading the assorted newspaper clippings. My parents must have felt that they were finally done with this ordeal when my dad headed north after the first verdict. And, as evidenced by their letters, now that he had been returned to jail, they were in a state of disbelief that this was happening to them again, regardless of his admission of guilt.

The words written and exchanged between them, after they found themselves back in the same situation, can come across as if they felt that they were the victims. However, knowing that they had just gone through one trial, I'm sure they were shocked, thinking that they were finished and ready to put this behind them.

What the newspaper articles don't say, and that I now know, is that the "charges of making improper advances to a 13-year-old boy" were brought forth by my uncle Buddy, who was married to my mother's older sister Betty, on behalf of my cousin, their son Robert.

York family home, Nashville

Tool shed where box of letters were found, Nashville

Dade County Courthouse & Jail

SIX.

The days were hectic as I prepared for the estate sale. Decisions had to be made, and I was blessed with having a family friend, who conducts sales professionally, to help me. In turn, she had ladies who helped her. One of the ladies shared with me that we went to the same church. I learned that her husband was deceased, and her son in jail. As I put two and two together, I realized that I had known her husband. In fact, I had known him intimately. He was not my first seducer, but came along later when I was a young teen. How awkward to hold that secret while she helped me go through our personal things, pricing them for the sale.

The box of letters stayed in my garage for several years and then moved with me. I could not bring myself to go through them. I'm sure there are those unable to understand my procrastination, but honestly, I don't think I was ready to come to terms with what personal secrets they held.

Fifteen years after my dad's death, a movie triggered a memory and my thoughts went to that box. I retrieved it from the garage. I began putting the letters in order by postmark, separating my dad's letters from my mom's. I also realized that there were additional newspaper clippings, cards from friends, and photos in the box which gave me even more insight as to the progression of events. Once everything was in order, I began to read.

It broke my heart when I read how my mother and father struggled for the two months he was in jail. Each night she would bring me to stand on the corner and wave to him. She would blink the car lights to let him know we were there and he would strike a match from his window, on the 21st floor, to signal he was watching. Eventually they came up with a code by the amount of blinks, or if the match went from side to side or up and down, to convey news. She was able to visit him for two hours each Sunday looking through wire and glass.

I was only two years old at the time, and as hard as I have tried, I have no recollection of any of this. Still there it is, in their own handwriting...our life and our struggles for me to read. The same scribbling that I easily recognize from past notes, postcards from their travels, grocery lists, checks, birthday and report cards of my youth, are now telling me a story. Unpleasant for sure, and often hard to read, but still, it is a part of my life, my family history.

November 29, 1946

Back row: *Guy Cutulo, unknown, Earl Culbreth, Ed Kaplan, Dr. C. Roy Angell, James York, unknown, Cecil Carroll, unknown*

Middle row: *unknown, unknown, June Broadway, Betty Broadway Morrison, Bob York, Joyce Broadway York, unknown, unknown, unknown, unknown*

Front row: *George Culver, Barbara Carroll, Robert Morrison*

FAMILY

Robert "Bob" York	Accused 34-year-old husband, father, insurance Salesman, and Boy Scout leader
Joyce York	29-year-old wife, mother, and former church secretary
Ron York	Two-year-old son at the time, and narrator of this story
Betty Morrison	Older sister of Joyce
Buddy Morrison	Husband of Betty and accuser of Bob
Robert Morrison	13-year-old son and victim
June Broadway	Younger sister of Joyce and Betty
Dave Doggart	Ex-husband of June
Bobbye Fortner	Youngest sister of Joyce, Betty and June
Bill Fortner	Husband of Bobbye

FRIENDS

Harry "D-Dad" Flynn	Close friend and proprietor of Lynn's drug store/luncheonette
Mimi Flynn	Dear friend and wife of D-Dad
Monnie "Brownie" Flynn	20-year-old son, fireman, former Scout
"Little" Harry Flynn	17-year-old youngest son, former Scout
Bud Stone	Friend and co-worker at Independent Life
Kat Stone	Wife of Bud
Susan Stone	Two-year-old daughter
Cecil Carroll	Vice-President at Independent Life's home office in Jacksonville, Florida
Lena Carroll	Wife of Cecil

U.L. Stewart	Brother-in-law of Carrolls, employed by Independent Life
Bobbie Stewart	Wife of U.L. and Lena Carroll's sister
Earl Culbreth	Cousin to the Carrolls, employed by Independent Life
Estelle Culbreth	Married to Earl
Bill Culbreth	Brother of Earl and pastor of First Baptist Church
Raby	Friend who appears to have helped Yorks financially
Dr. C. Roy Angell	aka "Preacher" of Central Baptist Church
Berdeaux Family	aka "24th Ave" folks, whose twin sons were Scouts
Guy Cutulo	aka "7th Street," accused former physical education teacher and assistant Scoutmaster
Addie Cutulo	Wife of Guy

LEGAL

Bill Pruitt	Attorney
Bill Pruitt, Jr.	Attorney
Mrs. Fay	Secretary
Judge Ben C. Willard	Criminal Court Judge
George A. Brautigam	State Attorney General

Friday 12 Noon
November 18, 1955

Hi Sweetheart,

Not knowing how long I'm going to be in here, I'll write you a note anyhow.

This is not exactly the way I want to spend much more of my life. It isn't nearly so bad as Jacksonville, but still I'd like to be outside. I try not to spend too much time thinking about you and Ron, because it nearly gets me down. Now don't misunderstand, actually I think of you all of the time. I just don't dare concentrate too much.

Friday Nite
Just another line tonight. I found out that the mail didn't go out until tonight. As I told you on the phone, I have talked to the doctors. It was pretty rough. One of the doctors didn't seem to believe that all of this was horseplay but the second was a little more sympathetic. I think that he had worked with kids and could understand. I sure hope I could get out of here by tomorrow. Well, I just don't know a thing so I will close. Please don't make a statement to anyone about anything.

Bill Pruitt Jr. was up this PM and said that they were trying to get the doctor to come on. I'm afraid that if he doesn't come soon enough, I'll have to stay here over the weekend and I sure hate that they have a TV here but no arm chairs. The iron benches get a little hard. However, I'll survive and I know this can't last forever. If I don't get out, they have a visitor's day Sunday but I'm almost afraid for you to come because it isn't too pretty a picture. Well, I don't know anything more so I'll get this in the mail, I hope.

All the love in the world to you and that sweet little boy. Hug his neck and see if he has a kiss for me.

Love,
Bob

Saturday Nite
November 19, 1955

I think my address is Dade County Jail 21-N, Miami, Fla.

Hello Sweetheart,

I had hoped that I could talk to you today but I couldn't get permission to use the phone. I thought that maybe Bill Pruitt would come by today and give me some information, but I guess that is asking too much. I guess that the doctors won't make their report until the first of next week. I guess the folks outside don't get in as big a hurry as the folks inside. I wish I knew what the outcome would be, although I guess that might not be good either.

I have seen two or three pictures on TV that made me think of Ron sitting in the big chair with his thumb in his mouth. I've got a red-hot headache tonight. However, since I can't run down to the drug store for BC, I'll just sit it out. This mail deal is like the Army. Everything going in or out is censored, but I guess that they have to do that. Honey, if this thing ever clears up, I don't think I ever want you and Ron out of my sight again. It takes something like this to make a guy appreciate his wife and baby more and more.

Baby, just hold your head up and get out and see some folks and keep smiling as I'm sure the good Lord will make a way.

Kiss my boy for me and have him give you a kiss.

Love,
Bob

P.S. I guess my friend, Buddy *(Brother-in-law)*, is enjoying this deal. I'll bet he checks every day to see that I'm still in.

Sunday
November 20, 1955

Hi Darling,

Honestly, I didn't know two hours could be so short as those two I spent with you this afternoon. Even standing on my toes didn't make it seem long. The balls of my feet are so sore I can hardly walk. Guess short people aren't supposed to go visiting and I'm not even very short.

Darling, you will never know how much good it did me to get to see you. Of course, I know you had your spirits up to try and bolster me up. From Thursday until Sunday seemed like an eternity. Honey, you will never know how I worried about you and your having to stay up there. I felt so guilty when I laid down in the nice soft bed.

The only thing I know about conditions in jail were what you had told me about that night in Jacksonville and I had nightmares just thinking about it.

Darling, everyone has been just wonderful to me and to Ron. Friday night Ron didn't want to come home from Mimi's with me and I said, "Honey, Daddy isn't here and you have to take care of Mommie." He looked at me and then hugged my neck and kissed me and said, "OK Mommie."

After leaving you today, I picked up the suitcase downstairs and it felt almost as heavy as it did when I went up so you can imagine how much stuff I had brought. Guess they thought I was trying to move you in for life.

Went by the store, as Mimi had asked me to take her to Shell's. But, when I got there she wasn't in the mood and I wasn't either.

Went by Mother's and Ron was asleep so I left him and asked the Stones to pick him up there.

Honey, you should have been here Sunday night. I practically met myself coming and going. Some man from across the street came over and wanted to look

at the house. Of course, I was a little leery of letting him in but finally did. His mother is moving down here from the north and he would like to have her in the neighborhood. However, he wasn't too elated over the house but said he would send her the details.

Jean Epperson called and we cried with each other for a while.

Then honey, and this sounds crazy, some man came to the door. He gave me his name and address – said he works for the *Herald* and comes home about 4:00 AM. Says the last five nights a wild cat has been prowling our property and Mr. James' property. Said it was a big one and was walking the wall last night. Suggested I call the police – which I did –and they said if I would call them when I saw it they would have a car here in just a matter of seconds but they couldn't send someone out just to search. The man I talked to was very nice. The fellow that came by suggested I leave the outside lights on if I went out at night. He said that Saturday night several of the dogs in the neighborhood were really barking when he went by. And they were, too, because they woke me up and I looked at the time and just figured one had gotten started and the rest of them chimed in. Boy! darling, you just don't know how I wished for you.

While that man was still here, June *(Younger sister)* came by. We had quite a nice talk about a lot of things in general. She explained a few things that made it easier to understand Betty's *(Older sister)* attitude. First, they have not taken Robert *(Betty's son)* to a doctor. Every time they talk about it he cries and says, "You think I'm crazy." Two, Buddy's *(Betty's husband)* upset because you were to receive no help and would be in the same situation again. I told June nothing that I minded being repeated so don't worry.

While June was still here, Mimi called and said she had visitors from 7th Street. *(Cutulo)* I was waiting on Ron but said I would be over later.

Then Kat called and said they were home and to come get Ron. He threw a fit and after much screaming we were on our way.

From there we went to Mimi's and had coffee. Nothing exciting – about the same. It was sorta depressing, and even D-Dad couldn't liven things up.

Well honey, it's mighty late and I guess by now you are trying to get some sleep. Honey, I know if you couldn't sleep good at home, you aren't getting too much sleep there. Don't worry too much. Try to look at the funny side of whatever goes on up there and maybe it won't be too bad. Guess people think I'm crazy because I was laughing about my visit to you – the clothes in the paper bag – standing on my tiptoes – shouting at each other so we could hear, etc. But honey, if I didn't laugh I would cry and I don't have your shoulder to cry on.

Guess you will talk with friend Bill *(Attorney)* tomorrow, I hope. Surely he can work out something. You know I will be here doing everything I possibly can. It can't last much longer.

Darling, you will never know how long these days are without you – when I can't see you or talk with you. But you can be assured that my thoughts are with you constantly. I love you very much.

When I kneel down to say my prayers at night, I miss your arm around me. But I know that even though we are apart that you are praying too. The Lord has been good to us in lots of ways and he will hear our prayers.

All my love,
Joyce

P.S. Ron even consented tonight to send you some kisses!

Betty, Joyce & June Broadway

Sunday PM
November 20, 1955

Hello Darling,

Well, you have been gone only two or three hours and it seems like a year. Honey, I just know that when you have something like we have that the Lord isn't going to keep us separated very long.

I really had to laugh when I got the bag of things that you brought. They had crammed all of the things in and the suit and pants looked like they were the bellows of an accordion. However, I hung them up and they will be OK by the time I need them, I'm sure. This has been the longest day I've spent yet. It seemed like a year all morning waiting on you to come and now seems that long since you left.

I was thinking about the doctors' names – if I saw a directory I could probably remember them but I'm not sure.

No supper tonight – wish I had those brownies that you baked. I'll bet they were good.

Tell old Ron that we will get him another piano some day so he can sing. It's pretty heartbreaking seeing those things we love so well going. But my darling, if you'll stick by me, I'll someday make it up to you or surely spend my life trying and it will be my pleasure to try to.

Well, I'm starting to think now that I'd better close – all my love to both of you.

Bob

Monday
November 21, 1955

Dearest Bob,

There isn't much to write about but I did want you to know I was thinking of you and just marking time until you will be out.

Ron slept until 8:30 this morning and was I glad!! Of course he will never do that when you are home. He insisted on having oatmeal for breakfast!! Honey, he misses his Daddy but seems satisfied with the explanation that you are working. Guess he thinks you sure have started working a lot more than you used to.

Honey, this morning I have sat glued to this chair by the telephone hoping to hear something. Finally around noon I called Pruitt and he called me back about one but the only thing he said was that they did know the names of the doctors and were working on the reports. He said he would probably see you this afternoon so I guess you know more about it than I do.

Mamie T. came by just before noon and got Ron to keep him today. She brought him back around 5:00. I was going to take him out to eat but that stinker wanted to eat dinner at home. So I fixed dinner and we watched TV while we ate.

Honey, I stayed up until 3:00 watching for the wildcat and finally fell asleep. So, if he came last night, I missed him.

Have had several phone calls today – the usual ones – Bobbie, Mother, Kat, etc. Cubbedge *(Scout leader)* came by and I thought he would never leave. He stayed nearly 2 hours. They are planning to reorganize the Scout troop and he wanted copies of all the records, forms, etc. I said I would have to get them 'cuz I wasn't much interested in bothering with it and wasn't sure just what you wanted him to have. They are also looking for a good Scoutmaster.

Fay Clark had her baby – a boy. I know you are real interested!

Honey, I have stayed home all day and done nothing. I did run the sweeper and then Ron crumbled brownies on the floor!!

Mrs. Fay called me today and was asking if I had seen you yesterday – how you were doing, etc. Then she started asking about the house – if we had any prospects – what we were asking, etc. I really cried poor mouth 'cuz I was afraid Pruitt was going to ask for more cash.

Honey, I called Raby and someone had told her we sold the piano, probably Bobbie Stewart. So I asked her if I could keep the money a few days until I knew what it would cost to get you out. She said alright but as soon as we can, I want to give her some money.

Late this afternoon Hildreth called and said some man had called her and said, "Why don't you call Joyce York." She didn't know who it was. So we talked a while and she was very nice.

Honey, I called Joe and told him if he would come by I would give him a couple of weeks on the insurance. It is a few weeks behind now.

I know all this stuff sounds silly with you up there but there really isn't much to write. I just live for a phone call from Bill Pruitt. Incidentally, I told him that I hate to keep calling but I go crazy when I don't hear anything and hate to leave the house for fear he might call. He said, "That's all right – call anytime you want."

Well sweetheart, it's getting late. Ron has already fallen asleep in your chair. He has been such a doll!! He wanted some cookies and wanted me to eat some. When I said I didn't want any he says, "I'll kiss you – you feel better."

Honey, know that we are with you every minute – loving you more and more. Maybe tomorrow we'll have good news.

Bushels of love,
Joyce & Ron

Monday Nite
November 21, 1955

Hello Darling,

Well, another day is about to end and I haven't heard a word from Pruitt. I suppose that I'll hear something tomorrow, I hope. I guess that maybe the doctors didn't work Saturday and maybe just made the reports today and maybe they will be in tomorrow. I'm doing lots of speculating but what else is there to do? I do wish that there was some way to get news though. It looks like that this mail must run about two days behind. So if I don't get out the letter tonight it might not get to you until after Thanksgiving. If not, I certainly want you and Ron to go to the Flynn's and have a good time. Don't worry about anything. Surely it will work out.

Honey, I just want to hold you close and be near to you so bad I can hardly stand it. I really am living every hour twice until I can be with you again.

I hope you get a chance to talk to Dr. Angell as he may be able to help some.

Be sure to call Raby if you get a chance and keep her informed.

I'm catching a cold – everyone in here has one. I've ordered some pills – guess I'll get them about Thursday. Well, hope that little old sweet boy is OK. By the way, you ought to go get your teeth fixed. Don't worry about the money because if would be cheaper to fix them now than later. Guess I'll close. I love you a million times. Kiss Ron for me.

Love,
Bob

Tuesday
November 22, 1955

Dearest,

If this letter doesn't make very good sense I wouldn't be surprised 'cuz I'm at the Flynn's. Everything is quiet now – other than the TV but no telling what will develop before the night is over.

Well darling, this has been another of those long days but I'm sure it has been even longer for you. Honey, I waited until noon and finally called Pruitt. Bill, Jr. said he was just going to see if the doctors' reports were in. I waited there until 4:00 and called Mrs. Fay. She said "no," but they promised to do everything possible so you could be home by Thursday. I really get aggravated but there is nothing I can do. Surely by tomorrow night we will be together again.

Honey, I can't seem to get my mind functioning to do anything. The telephone has been ringing constantly. I finally almost quit answering it this afternoon but then I was afraid it might be something important. It seems there are so many people that feel I ought to call and let them know what is happening. I really appreciate their concern but not knowing anything, they just want to talk!!

Honey, I finally got to the bank this afternoon to deposit that check on the piano. So if you have to write a check for the bond the money is there.

After I went to the bank, I rode to town and walked around a couple of hours – just looking! It sorta kept me occupied because I haven't been out of the house much.

Ron spent the day with Mimi. She came after him around 11:00 AM. He was so sweet this morning. I was sorta sick – must have been a virus or something. I had a terrific headache when I woke up and took a couple of aspirin and they made me sick. Ron insisted I had to eat breakfast. He kept kissing me to make me feel better. I was lying on the bed and he brought the hassock in and sat beside me. Then he would carry the hassock into the bathroom and get me a glass of water. Honey, so don't worry about us.

We had dinner at the Flynn's tonight. You should have seen Ron when I came in – he was a sight. Brownie had found an old bathing suit of Little Harry's which he put on Ron. It wasn't much too big either.

Saw Cecil Lanier in the bank today. He was rushing around getting ready to leave tomorrow. He gave me his address so we could let him know how things work out. Bob Lynch was with him. He had been visiting Nancy this week.

Honey, I wrote your Daddy a note today even though there really isn't much to tell.

Thought I would write this tonight even though I'm praying you will be out before it gets there.

Darling, this just can't go on much longer. I'm just no good without you.

I miss you and love you very, very much. Ron and I both send all our love and kisses.

Joyce

"Little" Harry, Harry "D-Dad" & Monnie "Brownie" Flynn

Tuesday Night
November 22, 1955

Hi Darling,

Well, another day and still no word. It really gets me down not to hear anything. I'm sure Mr. Pruitt doesn't have any idea what it means to have to sit here day after day and not get any word. If I'm not out or you have not heard from me by the time you get this – call Pruitt and ask him if he won't come up and talk to me for a few minutes even if it cost $10 dollars for ten minutes. I heard they may have visiting on Thanksgiving but I'm not sure. Honey, I can't help making some kind of plans so I just lay here thinking about you and Ron and I together somewhere. I don't care much about what or where but just to be together. I have learned so much since all this started. I knew I loved you but I don't think I had any idea how much. I know that the Lord has something in mind in all this and I'm convinced that somewhere down the line I didn't do what he told me. I don't know what it is he has in mind for me but whatever it is I'm going to do it if I ever get the chance.

Gosh, I'm beginning to sound like a preacher! Who knows?

Did you talk with Dr. Angell? It looks like I'm going to need lots of luck and I'm sure that people will do more for you than for me.

Honey, if the battery on the car gives you any trouble, put the charger on. The red wire goes on the terminal on the battery nearest the motor. The black one on the outside terminal. Then you flip the switch to 6 volts. If the motor doesn't register move the clips around until they are tight.

If you should get this letter Wednesday and call Pruitt, just explain that I'm anxious for news and that is why I'm asking for him to come up. As I said Sunday, we have given him so much money we can't afford to foul up with him because we couldn't start over.

Guess I'll close and send my love to you both.

Love,
Bob

Wednesday
November 23, 1955

My Darling,

I shouldn't be writing this letter now because I'm just not up to it, but I just had to. I would give anything in this world if I could just see you and talk to you. Everybody is so good but nobody will take your place. Honey, this has just got to work out because I can't stand it without you.

I guess by now you have talked with Bill, Jr. and know the news. I just can't believe it and told him what you had said about the examination. Maybe that will help some, but I just don't know.

Try your best not to worry because I know everything is going to work out. Our life together has been too wonderful to let something like this mar it. Every minute of every day I am right there with you. I realize now more than ever how much a part of you I am. Whatever happens, remember this is just a small part of our lives and there are bigger things ahead.

Honey, I can't bear the thoughts of Thanksgiving without you. It doesn't sound at all exciting to bake pies when you can't be there to enjoy them. I wish I hadn't promised to do it. I really don't want to go. I would like to take Ron out to dinner and we just be by ourselves. It isn't right without you. I keep thinking about what is one Thanksgiving when we have had so many happy ones and will have so many more. But honey, I'm going to bake pumpkin pie and you always said that wasn't my best so you won't miss anything.

Guess what I got roped into. This is really typical! Harry said Kathryn, at the store, couldn't bake the turkey so he wanted to surprise Mimi and would I bake the turkey and make the dressing!! So, you know me. I said yes. Now I'm sick over spending the day in the kitchen and you won't even be there to eat. But darling, I'll try to get the turkey done anyway.

Honey, I was so happy to hear from Carl, of course. I couldn't tell him much or probably anything that you didn't already know. I figured by now you had talked

with Bill, Jr. and knew there was nothing we could do until the hearing on Tuesday. Things don't look too good but I just can't get discouraged or I couldn't stand it. I have to keep hoping and praying that it is all going to work out like we want it.

Wayne Odom came by and said he would call around a couple of places about the car and may do some good. He was very sweet and very complimentary about all the things you have done for him.

Darling, Ron went to the nursery at church with Susan Stone. He was really delighted to go but I sorta hated to see him go.

Ron has really enjoyed his letter. He carries it around all the time. He wrote you a letter but I can't find it right now to send it. He talks about his Daddy all the time. This morning I was in the kitchen when he got up. He came in and said, "I went into my Daddy's room and he wasn't there." I started crying and he hugged me and said, "Don't cry Mommie, Daddy's gone to work. He'll be back." I don't mean to upset you but I want you to know how much we both miss you and love you.

Honey, my former boss called today and wanted to know why I hadn't called him. I told him he had done enough and I didn't want to bother him. Well, he said a friend had assured him we might be happy with his decision if he got to see you again. Of course, it is the thing we have been praying for all along.

I wrote to Independent Life several days ago. Had a letter today and they said we could make interest payments until the last of January. I had already sent two interest payments.

I paid Joe three weeks on the insurance. He came by yesterday.

I have taken care of the necessary bills to date so don't worry. Those things are all working out OK.

I guess I had better go get Ron. I have been at the store & ate supper at Lynn's.

Harry said that Joe came by our house to see if he could do anything. I'm just glad I wasn't home. Harry says Joe is 100% for you but if he can't tell you to your face I don't need to see him.

Passed Mary Frances Counts in the car today and she didn't speak. Oh well!!

Darling, I better close or you won't get this. I hope they have visiting hours tomorrow so I can see you.

Thanks for all the letters. They are wonderful.

All our love,
Joyce & Ron

Wednesday
November 23, 1955

Hello Sweetheart,

I just talked with Bill Pruitt, Jr. and he told me about the doctor's reports. I must say it came as a shock and yet I told you last Sunday I don't see how they could have decided anything from the examination they gave me. You know I have a theory that you might check up on. You remember I told you about the young doctor who seemed to know so much – I wonder if that is the one Robert went to? That would be just peachy. Bill said unless something happened good, I won't get out until next Tuesday for the hearing. And then who knows what.

Honey, I don't know but it looks like they are trying to stack the chips against me. If I have to go to an asylum they tell me you really have a time getting out of one of them. You are going to have to have a lot of courage and though I know it throws a lot on you, I want you to know that without you I'm afraid I'll go down like a drowning man. I miss you and Ron so much that I can hardly stand it but somehow maybe I will.

I haven't gotten any mail from you yet but I don't think that they give mail here but once or twice a week. Sure would help if they would let you hear more.

It looks to me like if they would give me a bond before *(during the first trial)*, they would again.

Well, darling, I'll close and hope this gets to you before too long. All my love to you and Ron.

Love,
Bob

Wednesday
November 23, 1955

My dearest Bob,

It is almost midnight but somehow I couldn't go to bed without writing you
another note. This all seems so unfair that we must go through this. I can't
understand why they couldn't let you out on bail, but I guess we must accept it and
pray that it won't be for long.

Honey, I told you about the letter from Independent in another letter but a little
more in detail. The board granted a term mortgage until January 25th when regular
payments would have to be resumed. I had sent one month interest. They credited
it as interest and said as of November 25th we would owe $63.30, which is the
interest payment and also some balance due on late charges. I am praying that we
can sell the house in the next month or so.

Speaking of selling the house, a woman came by and asked to look at it. She said
she had called the real estate office six times and they never returned her call. She
was very interested and acted like she was ready to move in. However, they own
a house in South Miami which they are trying to sell. She is going to bring her
husband back Friday to look at the house.

Darling, I am really very upset about Thanksgiving. I hate to think of going to the
Flynn's without you. I would like to just treat it as an ordinary day but I can't very
well get out of it. Honey, when I went to pick up the turkey, which Harry had asked
me to cook, he also had some sweet potatoes. So I am fixing the turkey, dressing,
gravy, sweet potatoes and pie. Doesn't it sound great to spend the entire day
when you won't even be there to enjoy it? Can't I get in the worst messes and then
complain? I know Harry probably thinks it will be good for me to keep busy.

I called tonight to see if maybe I could get to see you tomorrow but they said no.
However, I am going to call again in the morning just in case.

I went to get Ron from the Stones tonight and stayed and talked for a little while. It was nice to just get my mind off things. Darling, Bud is going to put the charger on the battery for me tomorrow for a while. It hasn't given me any trouble but I don't want it to and I know you said it was low last week.

I have all the bills, installment banks, etc. together and I'm keeping up with everything so don't worry about that. You have enough to think about. Honey, Henry C. called today and just wanted to know how things were and if there was anything new. He was very nice. Said he heard a rumor that someone had said they had heard he had loaned you some money to leave town. We had quite a laugh and I said I was sorry that he had been accused but he said not to worry that his shoulders were broad. I don't know what people will figure out next. They have had quite a picnic making up stories.

I hope you are getting my mail. I have a time trying to write with Ron and the telephone and I know they probably don't make good sense when you get them.

Hope you get that cold knocked out right away because you sure don't need to be sick now.

Darling, each minute seems like an eternity. The days are so long and the nights are even longer. I hate to go to bed and I hate to get up in the morning. Without you – this isn't living – it's just marking time. Even though the past nine years have been wonderful, I'm sure when this is all over we will have an even better life together. I think we have both learned a lot of things that I think will make us bigger and better and draw us closer to each other. Honey, you don't know how I need your love. I need your arms around me to make me feel secure. I feel so lost and helpless without you. I wake up in the night and look for you beside me.

I had a nice note from Allyne & Reeder Norman inviting me to eat Thanksgiving dinner with them. I thought it was so sweet.

I'll be up to see you Sunday so if you need anything or want anything you can write me or tell Bill Pruitt whenever you see him. I guess you could probably use another clean shirt or two and maybe some old pants. You know, you have almost everything you have now. Wish I had thought to have some of your clothes

brought from Jacksonville when the folks come this weekend.

I heard tonight that Earl and Estelle are expecting an addition to their family. Some news, huh?

Well darling, it is mighty late and I guess I am repeating myself. But remember that Ron and I are pulling for you. We need you so surely the Lord will see that. Honey, try to look on the bright side. This has just got to work out. I can't believe anything else. You have done too much good in your life to let this happen. I can hardly wait to see you again. Just wish I could touch you or hold you for a minute.

All our love, forever,
Joyce & Ron

Thursday Nite
November 24, 1955

Hello Sweetheart,

Guess that I have survived Thanksgiving. We did have a nice turkey dinner but no supper tonight. I'm sure that you all had a nice time. I'll bet old "Ronnie" ate plenty of turkey.

Time passed mighty slow today and I guess it was because I couldn't do anything but think of you and Ron. I still haven't gotten a letter from you but I guess I'll get some tomorrow.

I'll sure be glad to see this Sunday roll around so I can see you. You don't need to bring anything to wear except maybe a sport shirt. I've been taking care of my laundry.

I'm afraid I don't have much news, I'm just looking forward to Tuesday.

Honey, I love you and Ron with all my heart and I hope to see you mighty soon.

Love to you both,
Bob

Thursday/Thanksgiving
November 24, 1955

My Darling,

This is some Thanksgiving. I don't even let my mind wander to other Thanksgivings
and the wonderful times we have had. This is just another day as far as I'm
concerned and I'm looking forward to next Thanksgiving.

But you know, with all our trouble, we do have a lot to be thankful for. I'll admit it is
much easier to think about our troubles and we sorta have to search for the things
to be thankful for. But, you know, we do have a lot of wonderful, understanding
people who have meant a lot in our time of trouble. And Ron is certainly a blessing.
He has been a doll this morning and I have had lots of patience and let him help
me cook. He has been right by my side constantly. And of course, we do have our
house that we can sell that will help us financially. There are a lot of other things,
but I guess you have thought about them too. Most of all, I'm thankful for the past
nine years and the wonderful times we have had together. We have a world of
memories and a lot of things to be thankful for over the past years. And, honey,
we have a whole life time ahead with each other and our little boy. That is certainly
something to be thankful for.

This sounds like a lecture, but guess I am just a little melancholy today. I have
been home by myself all day. That Harry Flynn. I could wring his neck. If he hadn't
asked me to fix practically the whole dinner I wouldn't have had to stay home all
day by myself. Oh well, I shouldn't complain. I just ought to be thankful that I have
somewhere to go for Thanksgiving dinner.

This has been a very quiet day. Bobbie Stewart called and she was in the midst of
getting ready for Cecil and Lena. They are coming today from Jacksonville.

Bobbie wanted to write you but when I told her your address she said she just
couldn't but wants you to know that she is thinking of you and praying for you.
She doesn't call quite as often as she did and I am glad because it was a little
nerve-racking. There really wasn't much to talk about.

Cecil & Lena Carroll

Honey, tomorrow night is the Silver Anniversary party for Cecil & Lena. *(Joyce and Bob's anniversary was the same date.)* Even though we don't have the money, I thought I would take a couple of dollars and get a little something. They have been so good to us and I'm sure they'll understand if it isn't expensive. Darling, I talked with Guy today. They wanted to come by and bring me some turkey and dressing. I thought it was real sweet of them to think of me.

Talked with Daddy a minute and he was of course upset that I wasn't coming over there for dinner. I guess I'll try to go by later but I really don't feel up to it. They can upset me more than anybody I know.

I called again today just to be sure there were no visiting hours and couldn't help crying at the thought of not seeing you today. I read in the paper where you were going to have turkey. It will probably be better than what I have.

Honey, I know what you must be going through – not knowing what's going on. I've been thinking all day that maybe you would get a chance to get to a telephone.

I wrote your Daddy a note and tried to be very optimistic. There is no need to worry him but I know he worries if he doesn't hear anything.

Ron talks about you all the time. He wanted to buy you some candy today so you would have it when you came home. When I was crying this morning he said, "My Daddy be home in a minute." Darling, don't tell me he isn't smart.

Honey, we have just got to look toward the future and the wonderful life we can have together. I have to keep planning like that – so you do the same. This won't go on forever. We'll be together soon and life will be more wonderful than it has ever been.

I love you so very much. You are my life. Ron and I need you so hurry back to us.

My prayers are for you always and I know that whatever is right the Lord will do.

Sweetheart, I am living for Sunday when I can see you.

All our love, always,
Joyce & Ron

P.S. Ron said he had some sugar for you!!

Friday
November 25, 1955

Hi My Darling,

Thought I would try to get a note written before "my friend" wakes up. It is almost 8:00 AM and he is still snoozing. It was almost 11:00 before he went to bed last night. Then he was rather aggravated because he wanted to watch TV.

Honey, we really had a hilarious Thanksgiving – Ha! Ha! I had most of the dinner to take to the Flynn's. They wanted to eat at 6:00 and it was about 6:15 before I even got there. I worked nearly all day long on that stuff.

I parked the car across the street from their house and Ron started across and then started back. A car was coming and I gave him a little push. It pushed him into a car that was parked there and his nose started bleeding. Well, he and I were both in tears. I got him cleaned off and we ate. Ron ate a good dinner. He really clung to me though. He told everyone that he made the pies. He really was a doll.

Right after dinner I left because Harry was making me so nervous trying to be funny. I think they all understood how upset I was and will forgive me for the way I acted.

Darling, the usual bunch was there. Brownie had his girlfriend but other than that it was just family. Honey, I could hardly stand being there without you. It was almost more than I can bear separated from you.

After leaving the Flynn's, I rode downtown to mail you a letter. I looked up and wondered what you were doing. I figured you were probably in bed by 9:30 but I knew you weren't asleep. I knew you were probably thinking of us and it just killed me to be so close and not to be able to see you. I just believe that next year Thanksgiving will be a lot different. Honey, when we are together it is wonderful – even if we can't afford to buy a turkey.

Precious, I went to Mother's when I came back from town last night. Daddy wasn't there and I didn't stay long. They, of course, are upset but they are being wonderful. Daddy can't understand why I won't come home to stay until things are settled. But you know I couldn't. I told mother that all of his girls are hardheaded. You can't tell them a thing. I really am much better off here at home. Ron and I get along fine. As fine as we can without our Daddy. I think if I don't get to see you and hold you close, I'll just about pop.

Mrs. Mann from the the real estate company called this morning. They are going to have an open house here Sunday from 2:00-5:00. Sure hope it does some good. Honey, she said that they understand our situation and are doing everything possible to push the sale of the house. She said they had been praying for us and know everything will work out alright.

Last night about 11:00 PM the lady from next door called and asked if I was alone. She said she had seen me come in by myself a couple of nights. She wanted me to have her phone number so if anything happened and I needed them, I could call. I thought it was very thoughtful of her and it does make me feel better.

Darling, we had a letter from the telephone company with a little thing to put on our phone. The new number will be Newton 4-1639 as of December 3rd. I know it will take me a while to learn it.

Honey, I tried to call Pruitt this morning and he is out of town until Monday. Of course, I am very upset over that but will try to call him Sunday AM before I see you. I am being very nice to him and not meaning to push him but I just want to know what's going on. I'm concerned with what the procedure is from here. I know about the hearing but I don't know much after that.

By request, I have been trying to be a little careful in using names because I don't want to involve anyone but if this is any assurance – everyone is doing everything possible. Things don't look as bad as you probably think they do. Believe me – it will work out. I have even discussed the sanitarium angle and that picture is brighter than you think.

Honey, do you remember the man who came up and shook hands with you the day of the trial? You remember you tried to call him one day and he wasn't at work yet? Well, he is in the background but he is pulling 100%.

Norris Broadway with grandsons Brian Morrison & Ron

So many good people are working for you that surely it will be alright.

Darling, your letters came this morning and I was sick that you hadn't heard from me through Wednesday. The mail must be slow because I have written you every day.

Thanks for the information about the battery. It hasn't bothered me but I thought I would put the charger on. Bud looked at it yesterday but he wasn't too sure so I'll put it on tonight.

Kat called and asked me to go to the ball game tomorrow but I don't think I will. I just don't care about it. I think I would rather do something with Ron.

Honey, Raby called this morning and wanted you to know that she is thinking about you. I told her I was really concerned about the money but would get it to her just as soon as possible. She said she had already paid her taxes so not to worry about it.

Mamie T. called and wanted to keep Ron for a little while so I just took him over at 11:30 and I'm sitting at the stadium waiting on the bus. Thought I would go to

town and look around a little. You know how I love to shop – even if I don't have any money.

I'm real aggravated with Pruitt but I agree that we can't afford to start over again with someone else.

Honey, neither one of the doctors were the ones Betty talked to about Robert. And I have learned through June that one reason Betty has turned like she has is that she is a nervous wreck. Robert will not let them take him to a doctor. He cries when they mention it and says they think he is crazy. Betty told me they had so that I wouldn't worry and also, would quit asking her about it. However, she talked with one on the phone but it was not one of your doctors.

Please don't worry when you don't hear anything. It probably means nothing is actually happening. But there is some work going on. I am anxious to get to talk to you Sunday. It is hard to write and make myself clear.

I love you very much and it hurts that I can't seem to do much to help you. Believe me though, I try. All my love and my prayers are with you.

Love & kisses,
Joyce

Friday Nite
November 25, 1955

Hi Darling,

Well, Honey, I really had an exciting time today. I got 3 letters from you. That is the first mail I've had and I have already read them so many times that I have about worn them out.

Honey, I don't know if I wrote you or not but I was thinking about the doctors who examined Robert might be the same ones that I had. But from your letter I gather somebody lied to you about him being examined. In fact, I wonder how many other lies have been told.

Say, I'm sorry I haven't been there for the wild cat hunt. You be careful as they can be dangerous.

I sure am looking forward to Sunday when I can see you. If you get this in time, you might bring me a clean sport shirt.

Tell Pruitt, if you can, that I want to be able to talk to the judge at the hearing Tuesday. I certainly want to get in my 2 cents.

I wish we could move the house so we could give Bill Pruitt some more money so he will push a little bit harder.

Honey, just to have your letters gave me a thrill and I'm so proud that you are my wife. I don't think any other woman on earth could do what you have done.

It is really hot here tonight and as Ron says, I wish I could turn on the "conditioning."

Guess I'll close and send all my love to you and that sweet boy.

Love,
Bob

Friday
November 25, 1955

Hi my darling,

Well, another day is just about over and I'm a little closer to seeing you. It's strange that I should be so excited over seeing you under such circumstances. I grasp at anything. This has been such a long week. I hate to wake up in the morning because each day is the same. Darling, I didn't know life could be so empty.

Honey, you have been so wonderful about your writing. I treasure each letter and read them again and again. I know you don't have much to write about but you have really been marvelous!! I just hope that by now you have heard from me.

I really don't feel like doing a thing but just sitting. But, Ron is here and he demands. Besides, I nearly go nuts in this house without you. I wanted a big house but this is too big when I am by myself. It seems so empty.

Honey, I went to town for a little while today. I rode the bus down so I wouldn't have to pay parking. I had my hair cut thinking it would build up my morale. Then, I just shopped around. Kat is busy looking for a dress for their Christmas party. So, I thought to keep my mind off myself I would help look for dresses for her. I bought Ron a couple of books in the dime store that I thought I would save for Christmas.

Mimi took me over to that silver place on SW First Street and I bought a butter dish for Cecil and Lena. It is real pretty and cost a little over $3.00. I took the gift by Bobbie's and saw Lena for a few minutes. We had a good cry. I told her I would be thinking about them tonight at their party. I told her not to feel sorry for us and our anniversary. We have had seven wonderful anniversaries, plus the one you forgot, and we will have lots more. After all, this is just a day!! We can celebrate later.

Darling, I understand from the conversation that Cecil has received criticism for what he has tried to do for you. People seem to think that because anyone tries to help you they are condoning what you did. But, don't worry about Cecil. He is a mighty big person and can take whatever anyone gives.

I told Lena I would let them know as soon as we know something. She said they weren't worried about the car. It is alright as long as we want to leave it.

Honey, Ron and I cooked dinner at home today. He helped me with everything and then we ate in the living room and watched TV. I don't know what I'm going to do when you come home and we get back to eating at the table... but I'll be delighted!!

We stayed home tonight and watched TV. I sewed on some of Ron's pants... letting them down.

I was putting the charger on the battery tonight when the Pendergasts rode by. They stopped and he said it was alright.

Kat just called and said the party was a big success. She told me all about what everyone wore. She said Lena was just beautiful. I know everything was really nice. But we will really throw a party on our 25th anniversary.

Guess I will spend tomorrow trying to get the house straightened up – buy a few groceries – wash and iron.

I hope I'll hear from you tomorrow to tell me what to bring you Sunday. I guess a couple of shirts and a pair of pants. Wish I could get your dirty clothes.

Honey, it's late and there isn't much to write. We are just living for the day when we can all be together again. Ron quite frequently gives me a kiss on the back of the neck because "my Daddy told me to."

Darling, it is so lonesome without you. I don't see how this can last much longer. I love you so much. Didn't realize how much a part of me you are. I'm just no good without you.

Honey, each night I pray the Lord will do whatever is right for us and I know he will. There must be a reason for this and we'll see it someday.

I love you with all my heart and my life forever.

Joyce

P.S. Honey, Gerda Crane called to let us know she is thinking of us. Cubbage *(Scout leader)* called and said he came by. Thank goodness I wasn't here. Buster also called and wanted to know if there was anything he could do for me. Said he heard where you were and how sorry he was.

People are still thinking and praying for you. They all love you and want to help!!

Keep sweet as you are.

My mother begins her November 26th letter remembering a trip to Gainesville, Florida they took the previous year. She comments: "Funny how a year later former friends are now enemies."

My father's letter on the 26th shares the same memory saying: "Just a year ago on this Saturday we were in Gainesville living like human beings. Oh honey, won't it be wonderful when those days come again?"

My mother continued with: "Honey, around noon I just decided I had to get out for a while. So, we parked the car and Ron and I rode the bus to town. He had a big time. We looked around for about 30 minutes and he was so excited with all the toys and Christmas decorations. We didn't see Santa Claus because being Saturday it was crowded. We'll take him back someday. We had a good time and it didn't cost us anything but bus fare."

She added, noting the time of 11:00 PM, saying: "Here I am again. Goodness it sure is lonesome in this bed by myself!! I miss you so very much. I don't know when I miss you the most – in the morning when Ron would come and get in bed with us – or at noon when you would come home for lunch– in the afternoon when we would lay down – or around 6:30 when I keep looking for you to come home - or at night when I go to bed. Honey – so many times during the day and night I keep looking back at normal times and wistfully look at the future."

The Stones insisted she join them, along with four other couples, for dinner. She was hesitant to go but glad that she did. I stayed with my grandmother who said I fussed for a long time after my mother left. My mother confided in her letter to my dad: "He realizes something is wrong and he is so sweet. Tonight when I was getting dressed he wanted to help me with my belt. I let him try and then I started to fasten it and he said 'just a minute, honey.' Tonight when I picked him up he woke up just long enough to say, 'I call you up and you came and got me.' If you think I couldn't eat him up."

She tells my dad about the dinner and how each of the couples expressed their concern during the evening. Bobbie Stewart pulled her aside and gave her $10 and insisted that she take it. She concludes with: "Wasn't that thoughtful? Honestly darling, we will never be able to repay all the people for all the good they have done for us."

My father's letter from that day is hopeful for a hearing scheduled on Tuesday and finally learning where this latest charge is headed.

He closes his letter with: "Darling, you know those stories you read where it says someone's arm ached to hold someone else? Well, I always laughed at those things but never again. Mine are aching to hold you and to hold Ron so bad that I can hardly stand it."

Sunday Nite
November 27, 1955

Hello My Darling,

It was just mighty wonderful to see you today. I have but to see you to know what a lucky guy I am in spite of my troubles.

Honey, I sure have enjoyed having the paper today. It sorta reminded me of old times to read the paper on Sunday afternoon.

I was just thinking about Christmas. I sure wish that Ron could have a gym set but I just don't guess it would be wise to think about that now.

I'm sorry that I wasn't very cheerful today when you were here. However, I'm so tired that I don't seem to have very much control.

My darling, if I don't get out, I guess this will reach you Tuesday. It breaks my heart to write about it, but that is our anniversary. The day that marks the greatest thing that ever happened. I thank God for the wonderful times we have had together and I love you more than you could possibly know. I'm sure that there is going to be a very special place in heaven for people like you. That is, if there is anything or anyone else like you and I doubt that.

Honey, you keep our chins up and we will make it yet. In fact, I can just smell those South Carolina woods.

Guess I'll close and say to you that I love you very much.

Love,
Bob

P.S. Tell Ron... God bless you little boy

Sunday 10:45 PM
November 27, 1955

Hi Sweetheart,

Couldn't go to sleep without writing you a note. I know you are in bed by now but I know too that you are not asleep and I'll bet you are thinking of me as much as I am you.

Darling, it's funny what little things thrill me these days. I could hardly wait for tonight so Ron and I could go and wave. We were on the street about ten minutes. We got out and stood around, then walked to the corner and back. When we were sure you had seen us we got in the car. Ron was so thrilled. He said though that the windows were too small. They would have to make a big door so he could see his Daddy. He threw you a kiss and waved. I could have shot him because he wouldn't stand down. He said his feet hurt and he wanted to be carried.

Honey, we rode on downtown and Ron saw the big Santa Claus on Burdines *(Department store)*. We rode around the block so he could see it again.

Then we rode on out to Mimi's and Harry's. Mimi worked today and was dead tired. Harry came home and brought some turkey & ham and made sandwiches. Of course, it was a typical Flynn's special. There was no bread so we used hot dog buns and there was no mayonnaise. But since I hadn't eaten anything but a bowl of soup all day – it was good.

Darling, Ron sat in my lap coming home and helped me drive just like he helps Daddy.

Honey, Ron said something about he was going to stay at Mimi's and so I asked him who was going to take care of me. He turned to Mimi and said, "I better go home with my Mommie. She might be scared by herself."

Incidentally when we got to Mimi's Ron was so excited by waving to his Daddy that he couldn't tell her fast enough. He went through all the motions of waving and throwing a kiss.

It was good to see you today, Darling. I was sorry that I couldn't bring any news but I'll try to get Pruitt up there tomorrow. Honey, you have got to get some rest. Those bags under your eyes tell on you. I know you are nearly dead!!

Sweetheart, I would have given my right arm to have been able to touch you today – just to hold you close. It is misery to be so close and yet so far.

I went by Mother's for a few minutes this afternoon. Ron was still awake so I lay down with him for about five minutes and he went sound asleep. But did he give me a fit tonight when he saw me leaving him while he was asleep.

I rode by June's for a few minutes. She is busy packing to move home to Mother's this week. She didn't have much to say except that she babysat with Robert and Brian yesterday. Robert has the mumps and has had them since Wednesday. Betty and Buddy went to the ball game and out to dinner with Bill and Jenny.

Honey, I rode by the house and they had a big "open" sign but the place wasn't exactly flooded. In fact, there wasn't a car in sight. I thought I would call in the morning and see if they had any luck.

Darling, Ron and I went to church tonight. We got there a little late so I didn't see anyone except Joe Hiatt and I left during the invitational hymn.

Dr. Angell preached a good sermon on mastering life. He talked on being able to take prosperity and adversities. He said we should be content with life but not satisfied. He used Paul as an illustration – the hardships – trouble, etc. that he had in his life and yet Paul didn't complain but continued to strive. Then, of course, he concluded with the fact that we must have Jesus in our lives if we are to master our lives. That we must do what he wants us to do even though it isn't always what we think we should be doing for him. Darling, it really struck home and I wish you could have heard it.

I went in and sat down and pretty soon Mrs. Crane came and sat with me. I thought it was so sweet of her. She tried to take my mind off of things by complaining about everything but honey, she couldn't convince me. Everything was just beautiful! The stained-glass windows Ralph Ferrell had put in are really

June Broadway

out of this world. They are beautiful. John Rodgers sang "Face to Face" and it was very touching. There was a good crowd in church for a Sunday evening.

I'm about like you. I wish I could go to sleep and wake up Tuesday. I know tomorrow will be so long. In fact, every day is long without you. I guess something terrible has to happen sometimes to make you realize how much you love someone. I know, darling, that I knew I loved you but had no idea how much. You are everything to me. I just can't carry on without you so I know this will come to an end soon and everything will be alright.

I didn't realize how much space you take up in this big house but it sure is empty without you.

Darling, say a prayer for me some time that I can be of some good to you. I feel so helpless. Believe me though, I love you with all my heart.

Keep sweet for me.

Yours forever,
Joyce

Monday Nite
November 28, 1955

Hello Sweetheart,

I've been hanging on the door all day hoping to hear from Bill Pruitt. Not a word. I sure hope that tomorrow will bring the hearing so that we will have some idea of what is going to happen.

This has been a pretty long day and I have constantly thought of our anniversary tomorrow. I got your letters on Friday and Saturday and was glad to get them. I almost wanted to jump out the window when you reminded me that I had forgotten last year's anniversary. It makes me so ashamed because it was so typical of the way I have forgotten to do other things for you that I should have done. If I hadn't been so busy thinking of other things I would have done better.

Baby, I'll sure not let anything come between my love and thoughts of you again if I just have the chance.

I'm sure hoping that I get to see you tomorrow.

I thought I saw you and Ron down on the street last night. It looked like you were walking along the street from the railroad toward the bookstore. I tried to make a light but it didn't look like you saw me.

Honey, if I don't see you by the time you get this, I hope that Mimi has been able to get a little anniversary present to you. I have been trying for 3 days to get word to her but I'm not sure I'm getting through.

I'm sure that she'll attach the same importance to the brand as I do. I remember the first bottle sent to Ridgecrest. Do you? I knew then that you were somebody special and even more now I know that you are doubly extra-special. I hate to think of not being able to give this to you personally but you never can tell.

Well, I'll close this and send it with all my love.

Bob

8:45 Saw you and Ron... Good!

Tuesday
November 29, 1955

My Dearest Darling,

Well, this is our day! It has even more meaning today than it had nine years ago. Sweetheart, it grieves me to think of your being where you are and there isn't a thing I can do to get you out. Who ever thought that this could happen to us?

They say that when things start off bad they end good. So, even though this year our marriage isn't off to a very good start, I know that it will end even bigger and better than ever before. We have a lot of wonderful memories to keep this day alive and make it precious to us. All those good memories will wipe out this one bad day.

Precious, I heard your Bob White whistle this morning, but couldn't locate you. I am so glad that I did get to see you for a minute and kiss you. If we could just be together this could be a lot easier even though it would be bad enough. Being separated like this is agony. I think of you constantly and wish that I could just talk with you for a little while.

I'm mighty proud of you and the way you are holding up. You looked so nice this morning in your brown suit. But, you looked so out of place with those other fellows. It was like a nightmare and I couldn't believe it was you.

Honey, I was so confident that you were going to be out today that I didn't even write you last night. Isn't that terrible? Please forgive me for not writing but I just felt like everything was going to be alright and we would be together.

Ron was so thrilled at going down to see the big building where his Daddy was. He couldn't understand why he couldn't go in and see you or why you were there. He waved and threw you kisses. He was hollering "Hey, Daddy," at the top of his voice. I know people on the street were wondering what was going on. He was a little hurt because you didn't answer back but I explained that you were answering but you were up so high that he couldn't hear you.

Darling, Pruitt is rather confident over the final outcome, but he is just afraid of the time element. He is trying to rush things as much as possible because I think he is as tired of it as we are. I'll try to get him up to see you to let you know what is going on.

I worry about you in the cool weather. I hope it isn't too cold up there.

The letter I got today was mighty wonderful. If I had my life to live over, I'd do the same thing again. I'm glad that I married you nine years ago today and I'd do it again in a minute. Darling, I believe we have got something rich in our love for each other and regardless of what may come or go, we will be happy. You are everything to me. Without you my life is nothing.

Ron and I miss you more than you can ever realize. It just isn't fun doing anything without you. I try to do some things for Ron's sake but it isn't easy.

Remember that we love you and that it won't be long before we are together again.

All my love,
Joyce

P.S. Tell my friends up there hello and thank them for helping you keep your spirits up since I'm not there to do it. Let me know if I can do anything for them.

Tuesday
November 29, 1955

Hi Sweetheart,

I sure got a thrill being able to hold your hand for a minute and be able to kiss you. Honey, it looks like we just got another disappointment this morning. I'm about to reach the point where I've had about all the disappointments I can take. In fact, I guess I might as well give up and quit thinking I'll be able to get out anytime soon. I know that sounds bad but I think we might as well face realities. You might tell Pruitt that if *(State Attorney)* Brautigam decides to go on that, if he can get me out on bond without it costing us too much, to do so. Then maybe I can wind up my affairs and get ready for whatever may come.

Honey, in the excitement this AM, I signed something for you and have no idea what it was. Don't do anything with whatever it was until you can let me know unless you definitely think it's right.

About the Hudson: I think that we ought to get the final word before we do anything. And besides, why does the credit union want $300 – I don't owe that much, do I?

Before you ask Cecil to send down the retirement check with him, see if they will extend it anyway. If not, let them send it on.

Honey, this day means a lot to me and about 8:23 tonight, when we said "I do," I'll be thinking so much about you that I don't know if I can stand it. I sure love you, baby. You should have heard the fellows down there that saw you say how pretty you are. It made me proud.

Honey, if things don't work out for me to get out Thursday, ask Pruitt to get word to me so I'll know what to expect.

Well, guess I'll close and go take a look out the window. I love you, dear, and am with you in my thoughts every minute. Many happier returns of the day.

All my love to both of you,
Bob

Bob & Joyce with Dr. C. Roy "Preacher" Angell

Tuesday
November 29, 1955

Hi Darling,

I am still downtown but wanted to get this note written and mailed today in hopes you will get it tomorrow.

Honey, everything is going to be alright in the end. The main thing Pruitt is trying to do is hurry it up. We made a couple of visits when we left you. You know that he knows his way around!

Someone had already beat us to the punch on the visiting and so there will be some investigating. However, Pruitt isn't worried so don't you worry. I know this time isn't very pleasant for you but honey, just think of the future and this won't last long. The Circuit Court moves a little slower than *(Judge)* Williard's court but if you can just hold on the future is going to be much brighter. I wish I could explain more but it is best that I don't. Just have faith and everything will work out. Everyone is doing all they can. I know you can't realize that but believe me it is true.

Honey, I'll write to you when I get home but I wanted to get this in the mail.

I'll hold the Credit Union off this week until we see how things work out.

I hope you aren't cold up there. The weather has turned real cool.

Sweetheart, write me and tell me if you need anything – in case you are still there Sunday. Do you need a sweater? What kind of books do you prefer? Magazines?

Happy Anniversary, darling! We'll have lots more ahead!!

Stay sweet as ever – I love you.

Yours forever,
Joyce

Tuesday
November 29, 1955

My Darling,

I wish I could put into words the things that are in my heart. It is just too full. I love you so much. I know you must be the most thoughtful husband that ever lived. Honey, when Mimi gave me your cards and note and the bottle of Evening in Paris perfume, I thought I could hardly stand it. I could hardly wait until time when I could wave to you.

Sweetheart, I've thanked the good Lord many times for sending you to me and I did it again today when I saw you. I guess it takes trouble sometimes to make people fall to their knees. I am so thankful for the wonderful years we have had. You know, we have had a few difficulties and misunderstandings but I guess considering everything, they have been very few. Those wonderful memories have made this experience easier.

Some of these people who can't understand why I haven't left you surely must not have in their marriage what we have.

I know this sounds like a jumbled up mess but what I'm trying to say is "Happy Anniversary, Darling." I love you with all my heart and I'm already looking forward to next year when we can really celebrate!!

Honey, Pruitt is very encouraging in his talk. The only thing is that he is trying to get the trial as soon as possible. I hope and pray that something will happen this week. I know you must be going nuts. I think I am losing my mind so I have a small idea of what you are going through.

This afternoon I left Ron at Mother's for a nap and then came on home and called Raby and Bobbie. I hear Raby is on a binge and I'm about to believe it. She wants when this is all over for her to take you to her cabin in Kentucky. She didn't even invite me. Doesn't that sound exciting? Honestly she is mighty good-hearted but she is a screwball. She talked over an hour yesterday and I sorta feel obligated to listen to her. I wired your Daddy this afternoon but just told him there was nothing definite yet

and he still couldn't see you but I would write him details tonight. If you want him to come down just tell me and he will come in a minute.

Darling, I ate supper with Mother and Daddy. June was there and it was quite an affair. Everything was alright but we acted almost like strangers.

All the Flynns were very nice tonight. The card they got was beautiful but the sweetest thing was the note you sent. Honey, you shouldn't have worried about getting me something. You have enough on your mind. But I love it and it sure brings back lots of memories.

I wish you could hear Ron holler to you each night. He drew a picture of the big building where his Daddy is and I am enclosing it. Darling, you know each night I hate to leave Flagler Street. But, of course, I know I can do you no good just standing there. If I could send semaphore maybe I could at least tell you that I love you. But we look forward to those few minutes that are ours.

Talked with Guy and Addie *(Cutulo)* a few minutes. Did you know he is going to have 3 separate trials? They are pretty blue and discouraged. He has been working delivering telephone books.

Honey, there isn't much to write but to remind you how much we love you.

Ron has given me lots of kisses to save for his Daddy, so hurry home to collect.

We love you,
Joyce & Ron

Bob & Joyce, November 29, 1946

Sweetheart:
    Remember the first bottle of
this? It said "I love you" just like
this one does. Thanks for being my
wife.   Love Bob —

Wednesday
November 30, 1955

My dearest darling,

If there is a hell on earth – this must be it. Honey, I know the Lord won't give us more than we can stand but I'm afraid he thinks I'm stronger than I am. I feel so helpless and so lost. I would give anything in this world to be able to get you out. I feel so guilty because I can ride in the car or walk on the street or do whatever I want to. But sweetheart, nothing has a meaning if you cannot share it with me. I don't want to do a thing but just sit.

Honey, I wanted so bad to be able to tell you something tonight but 21 stories *(21st floor of the Dade County Jail)* is a long way up. Everything is going to be alright. The suffering you are going through now is the worst of it. From here on it is going to be better. Pruitt was working on every lead possible today but there was nothing definite. Something has just got to happen tomorrow. He told me to call whenever I feel like it or want to know anything.

Darling, I have always been so thoughtless and selfish all my life but I believe this will teach me to be more considerate and understanding. You will never realize how much I love you but I do because I hurt and suffer with you. I actually feel more a part of you than I ever have before. We are as one – believe me. I know you must feel alone and lost but don't, because you will never be alone.

Harry has a lead or two that may develop into something wonderful. I'm holding my breath. There are lots of good things being said and done for you so just hold on a little longer.

I stayed home all morning hoping and praying something would develop. Finally, I rode out to see about Ron's shots and they said he didn't need any. So, that's that for a while anyway.

Then there was a picture show *"The African Lion"* by Walt Disney and it was playing at the Coral. We saw the news, cartoon and a short. By the time the picture came on Ron's eyes were about to blink shut, so we left.

Honey, U.L. called and said you got a bonus this week... $165.00. Isn't that wonderful? It's like a gift from heaven. He said he would deposit it for me.

Sweetheart, I felt so blue tonight. If I could just have had you with me it would be so much easier.

I looked through the ads today and thought I would look for a job. There ought to be something I could do temporarily and still make some money. I hate to go to work and not be free in case there is anything I can do for you. Maybe I will look around tomorrow anyway. Someone has got to start making some money in this family. The hours are so bad at Burdines *(Department store)* that I don't see how I can do that with Ron and I hate to go to work in an office and maybe quit in a week or two. Oh well, something will work out.

Last night in the night Ron got up and got in bed with me and I let him stay there. It felt good to have him close – even though I didn't sleep too good. I guess he was cold or maybe he is as lonesome as I am.

Ron keeps asking for his Daddy and wanting his Daddy to go places with us. It just tears my heart out to hear him hollering "Hey Daddy," each night. I just wish you could hear him.

Honey, if something doesn't happen soon I will lose all of my friends. My disposition definitely isn't improving. Sometimes I think I'll scream if I have to talk to anyone and then I think about you and I know you would give anything to be able to talk with some of your friends.

I love you so much that I know the Lord is going to see us through and we'll be together soon.

Love always,
Joyce

Please allow me to repeat my mother's words from her letter of November 29th, 1955.

"Darling, I ate supper with Mother and Daddy. June was there and it was quite an affair. Everything was alright but we acted almost like strangers."

This was the evening of my parents' ninth wedding anniversary. It should have been a romantic dinner for two, but with my dad in jail, my mother dined with her parents and her recently divorced younger sister.

Many of my mother's letters dealt with day to day life as she tried to find normalcy for her and for me. But her life was anything but normal. Articles concerning the events of my dad's arrest were in the local paper and reported on TV news programs. At this point, there was probably not a friend or acquaintance in Miami that did not know the details of the arrest. Even strangers were aware of the two Scoutmasters and the accusations against them.

Wanting to remain independent, my mother did not move us in with her parents as they had asked. However, her younger divorced sister did move back home. I can only imagine the tension around that dinner table that night.

She was struggling to pay bills and care for me while thinking each Tuesday or Thursday his case would surely come to court and be settled. With each passing week and with little or no explanation, the court system seemed to stall in regards to my father's case.

Each night my mother and I would be on the sidewalk in front of the jail waving to my father as he watched from his window on the 21st floor. The letters indicate we could barely see him until he struck a match. But for a brief moment a bright light in the night sky would illuminate him. He mentions several times that the striking of the match from top to bottom was his way of saying "I love you." However, the lit match going from side to side would indicate he had heard news concerning his case. Likewise, my mother would flash the car lights once if she had heard promising news. Or not at all if something fell through or to signify there was no news to share. Although neither would know what the other had heard until they received a letter or were able to talk on Sunday, they could at least communicate that something was in the works.

Thursday
December 1, 1955

Hello Darling,

Sweetie Pie is taking a nap and while things are quiet I thought I would drop you a note and let you know I'm thinking of you. I imagine most of my letters don't make very good sense because it is a little difficult to concentrate with Ron talking.

Honey, I know you must feel like you are living again since Pruitt was up to talk with you. I was so thankful that he went up. He had called me earlier and told me the news and I asked him to please go to see you. He said he would and then I called him around noon and he said he had talked with you.

Last night I had decided that I was going to just insist that he go talk with you whether he knew anything or not – or maybe send Bill, Jr. So it was a relief when he called.

Darling, the letter I got today was written on Tuesday and it was so sweet. I know you are worried about my handling the finances but I'm not doing anything drastic.

The paper I had you sign was just in case I needed to get your retirement because I figured Pruitt would charge me if he made a special trip.

This is the story. I was afraid if it went to Circuit Court that it would drag out and you would lose your time with the company anyway. So, if they were going to send your retirement, the credit union wanted to be sure to get their money out of it.

I have all the bills paid up to date. I paid on the piano and the air conditioner today. We got a notice from Pat of $6.31 due on your camera insurance. Other than that, I think we are alright.

Honey, I had U.L. *(Stewart)* pay our insurance up to date with Joe. You see, when the bonus came in, U.L. said Joe would probably know about it and he has done some talking around the office about being afraid he is going to have to lapse it. You see, it seems the Hiatts have done an about-face in their attitude so I didn't want to give them something to talk about. I hope you approve.

106

Ron and I have stayed home all morning. The TV has been giving us a little trouble. Sometimes we can't get any sound. I have really just sorta messed around today and accomplished nothing.

Honey, I wrote Cecil and explained everything and asked if it were possible to hold things up for a week and if he could use you the next week and where. Maybe I will know something to tell you Sunday.

Also, I wrote your Daddy and told him the latest. I asked him please not to write or talk with Raby about it because I understand Raby talks around a little and Pruitt told me not to tell anyone. I hope he will understand.

I don't know whether your Daddy will decide to come down this weekend or not, but whatever he decides will be alright.

I know you have probably been freezing to death. It has really been cold. The gas heater isn't much good in the house. It heats that back bedroom, bath and part of

the dining room but the hot air really doesn't circulate much. But I have been using the little electric heater and for what time we are home it serves the purpose. Boy, I sure don't like cold weather.

Darling, I hope you write me something about what to bring you Sunday. I am having your suit and shirt cleaned but will probably bring just the shirt unless I hear different.

Honey, let me know anything you think of that I should do. The brakes aren't too good on the car and I thought about having Jack check them but I haven't. I sure would hate to spend $100 having them fixed but if we are going to keep the car, it may be necessary.

I think I will go ahead and mail this and write you again later. I want you to get this so you won't be worried about my spending all your money. Ha! Ha!

Keep sweet and hurry home.

All our love,
Joyce & Ron

P.S. I just had a wire from your Daddy saying he would arrive at 10:45 tomorrow morning. He had already left Richmond when I got the wire saying he will be up to see you Sunday.

Thursday
December 1, 1955

Hi Darling,

Looks like it goes on and on doesn't it?

I saw Pruitt this AM and he told me that he had told you what he told me. Boy, that's some sentence, isn't it? I don't know whether it looks good or bad. I haven't seen the doctors yet but sure hope to tomorrow. You better write Cecil, I guess, and ask him what he thinks considering the fact it might wind up next Thursday. Sorta hold on and stall everything until I talk with you Sunday. By the way, bring me that pair of pants out of the back bedroom closet. I don't think I need anything else.

Matches are just a little scarce so if I don't use too many don't be alarmed.

My darling, I'm just in a tizzy to see you. I love you so much! We'll never be apart for more than a few hours again if I can just get to be with you again. Honey, try to have a little party worked up for Ron if you can. Of course, I hope to be out before then, but you never know.

It would be a good idea to remind Pruitt that the 7th Street *(Cutulo)* deal is coming up Monday or Tuesday. In fact, I would call them and tell them that I'll be there Tuesday just so they could change their date if they wanted to. I don't think either one would be helpful.

I have met a rather wealthy fellow in here who has a perfume business in New York and he is interested in giving me a job selling perfume. He says they pay $250 a week and bonuses. There is some traveling in it. Sounds like a good deal. You know it pays to have something in the mill. We may need to work out something.

I haven't heard from you since Monday, but I hope to get some letters tomorrow.

Honey, just keep remembering that I love you with all my heart and soul. Kiss my little boy for me.

Love,
Bob

Thursday
December 1, 1955

Hi Darling,

There isn't much to write tonight because I wrote you this afternoon but I couldn't go to sleep without dropping you a line.

Honey, I feel so helpless when I go down to see you each night. I wish I could just talk with you or send you a message. But you know that I love you. I know you are up there watching me and wish I knew how to express myself long distance. But those few minutes are precious to me. I wouldn't take anything for them and wouldn't miss them for the world.

Darling, Mimi called right at suppertime and insisted that we come eat black-eyed peas, rice and cornbread. It was mighty good and Ron really put on a show. He was busy talking about Santa Claus. He kept trying to tell us something he was going to get and was very disgusted when we couldn't understand. Finally, Brownie guessed records and sure enough he was talking about a record player 'cuz he went on to explain about putting a record on and pushing a button.

Every night when we leave you we ride by to see the big Santa Claus. He is getting excited about Christmas and wants to have a Christmas tree "my own self."

I had a wire from your Daddy late this afternoon saying he would be in at 10:45 in the morning. I am a little upset about it because you know what a poor hostess I am. Besides, he will want to go to see you Sunday, I'm sure, and when I've waited all week for two hours with you, I'm very selfish about sharing it. So, Honey, if I don't come it's not because I don't love you but if he has come all the way from Richmond, I guess he is entitled to see you. Besides, I am sure you will be glad to see him.

Ron and I went to the grocery store and then came on home. He watched TV while I put up the groceries, made your Daddy's bed, etc.

Honey, that boy of ours is really a doll. When I get upset or something goes wrong he says, "I want my Daddy to come home."

I had quite a talk with the real estate man today. He said he just isn't making any headway with selling the house at $20,000. Really, he says $18,500 is a big price. He said it would move pretty fast at $17,000. So we had quite a talk and he explained a lot of things which sound very logical. He says the house is not attractive from the outside. The down payment is large and the monthly payments are large. He said people with that kind of money are not interested in a made-over house. He said he didn't mean to be tearing the house apart but was explaining why they were having difficulty. He was very nice. I can explain it better when I talk to you.

Darling, there is nothing much to tell so I'll close. I love you, my darling, and I'm looking forward to holding you in my arms soon.

All our love,
Joyce & Ron

Friday
December 2, 1955

Hi Sweetheart,

Another week is almost over and it seems like a year. Darling, I used to think time just flew by but it sure does drag by these days. Each day is like an eternity. I wait all day for the phone to ring with some good news – for the mail to come with a letter from you – and for 8:30 when we can wave to you. To some people they may seem like awfully little things but they are so important for me.

Well honey, your Daddy arrived this morning. We are really have a great time doing nothing. He is driving me insane doing nothing. We just sit here and look at each other. He wanted to go see Pruitt and I told him to do whatever he wanted to but I didn't think he could tell him any more than I had. I didn't try to talk him out of it but he finally talked himself out of it and I was really glad because I didn't see any reason for him to bother Pruitt for nothing.

He is waiting right now for Dr. Angell to call him back. I hope he does.

Darling, you'll never know how much I treasure each letter from you. They are so sweet. I know how difficult it must be for you to write since you aren't doing anything very exciting. But your letters are just wonderful.

I don't know what will develop with the company but it will all be for the best either way.

Honey, I've known for a long time that the Lord had given you an abundance of talents and that surely he could use you in more ways than you were serving. I don't know what he had in store for us but I'm sure he will lead the way. I wish we could be together to talk about it and pray about it. You know that whatever you feel is right will be what I want for you. I know that he wants our lives whether it is for full time service or just to be a full time Christian. I know we have slipped in lots of ways from what he would have us do but I know too, that he forgives and forgets and will show us the way to a richer fuller life. And I know how wonderful that life will be because we have each other. You know we are both pretty hard-

headed and the Lord knows he has to yell mighty hard for us to hear. But he can let up now.

If we could just talk things over and be together, I know we could work our lives out so that we would be happy and the Lord would be happy.

Honey, this has taught me a lot of things. I hope from now on that I can be a better wife and mother. I believe the Lord will show me the way. I know with your understanding and patience I can't fail. Honey, sometimes I wonder how you have put up with me.

Guess what? The bank statement came today and it balanced!! Isn't that a miracle? Wonders will never cease.

We got a form today to fill out for the Homestead Exemption. I'll talk with you Sunday about it. I guess I can sign it and send it in.

Honey, there isn't much to write so I'll just say that I love you and I'm praying earnestly that the Lord will show us the way He would have us go.

All our love,
Joyce & Ron

Friday
December 2, 1955

Hello Sweetheart,

These days roll around. In a way they drag mighty slow and in a way, when I think about Ron's birthday and Christmas, it seems like they are moving sorta fast.

I thought sure the doctor Bill Pruitt talked about would come by today. I'm afraid that if he doesn't come soon it will throw the thing later.

Baby, you said something about me praying that the Lord would let you help me. My darling, that is one prayer he has already answered a thousand times. You are like a fountain to me. When it looks as black as the inside of a hole, I have but to think of you to bring me back. You have no conception of what you mean to me. God gave me about the greatest gift he could give when he gave me you.

I enjoyed so much what you said about Dr. Angell's sermon. If you talk to him, tell him that he is a wise man and that I am setting my goals a lot higher in life that ever before.

8:30 is getting to be quite a highlight. Several of the guys are as anxious to see you as I am.

I sure hope the house will soon move. Be sure to try to handle it so that Pruitt doesn't get too much if I'm not available.

Well, guess I'll close with all my love to you and Ron.

Love,
Bob

Friday 10:30 PM
December 2, 1955

My dearest,

Seems like I just can't get to sleep until I have written you a note to say good-night. Somehow this is the most lonesome part of each day. I feel so alone and lost. I hate to go to sleep and I hate to stay awake. Darling, each day is like an eternity. The hours just creep by.

Today has been especially bad. You know I have always had difficulty carrying on conversation with your Daddy. So most of the day we just sat and talked a little but mostly just stared into space. He did go down and talk to Pruitt and feels a lot better. Pruitt is so confident that it gave him assurance. I was surprised that Pruitt would take so much time to talk with him but he probably thinks he has some money.

Three Generations

I'm awfully selfish and I know your Daddy is anxious to see you, but I sure did hate to share our few minutes tonight with him. Guess that is terrible and I try not to feel that way but honey, when it gets this close to Sunday and a chance to see you, I get so impatient.

We rode around and around tonight waiting for time to see you. When I finally saw the light as we went by, I could hardly wait to park the car.

Darling, we went to Sears tonight and your Daddy bought Ron an orange flannel shirt and some brown pants. Ron wanted the orange shirt because it matched my orange dress.

Ron has really eaten your Daddy up and I know it is because he misses his Daddy so much. But it won't be long until we are together again.

I was reading the Sunday School lesson and wished you were here so we could talk about it. I am enclosing it because it meant so much to me and I think it will to you.

There isn't much to write tonight. You are in my thoughts constantly. I love you with all my heart, darling. Looking forward to holding you close soon.

Yours,
Joyce

P.S. Your letters are full of such flattery that I'm going to be mighty hard to live with!!

Saturday Nite
December 3, 1955

Hello Sweetheart,

Another day – they sure are long ones, aren't they? I was tickled to see Daddy this PM. It was pretty hard to see him like this. I appreciated him coming down and I guess he felt better about it. He told me of his conversation with Pruitt. It is most encouraging yet I'm afraid to build up my hopes too much.

Honey, I wish you could have come up today. I'm sorta glad that Daddy came today so you could have all the time tomorrow. I am just counting the minutes until I see you.

Daddy said that he was going to check on the car with Cecil when he goes to Jacksonville tomorrow. He said that he would have it fixed. But I want only the minimum of work done on it and if it costs very much at all, I don't want anything done on it.

My darling, I miss you so much and thought that today would have been a good day for us to go Christmas shopping. Ha!

Honey, I don't know much of anything to write tonight. I just seem to be sorta of a blank. Guess I'll be able to say lots of things tomorrow. Just keep remembering that I love you with all my heart.

Keep being my sweet wife and you can know it means all the world to me.

Kiss my little boy for me.

Love,
Bob

James "Jim" York

Robert "Bob" York

Sunday Nite
December 4, 1955

Hi Sweetheart,

Seems to me like it has been about 2 days since you were up this afternoon. You sure did look pretty. Boy, what wouldn't I give to be able to squeeze you and have a good kiss.

I am beginning to have a feeling that Tuesday will see us together again for a while anyhow. Honey, if I do get to get away, I sure want us to get that house sold so you and Ron can get on up there with me. I don't think I will last too long anywhere without you.

This one thing I want to say though, Honey. If it doesn't go like we want it, I want you to be strong for both of us because Ron will need you so much. I do believe though that the Lord will give us our life together.

You said something in your letter about me being worried about you handling the money. Honey, I don't worry about your ability at all. The only thing I'm afraid of is someone trying to put pressure on you. You'll just have to be strong and I know you are that.

Please go ahead and get a record player for Ron if you can find one that is the right price. You might try Masters of Miami and some of the other cut-rate houses. Wish I could be there to help you pick one out as I know it will be lots of fun.

One thing we ought to have coming after the first of the year will be a sizable income tax refund. This being out of work so long will sure put me in a lower income tax bracket.

Well, honey, I'll close because there is not much news here. I love you more than you know. Kiss Ron for me and tell him to hug your neck for me.

Love to you both,
Bob

P.S. If you haven't yet, don't say anything to Guy.

Monday AM
December 5, 1955

Hi Darling,

Well, I thought that I wouldn't be writing you any more for a while but it looks like everything is against us. I just don't think I can stand any more disappointments.

On top of everything else, the Judge has to get sick. I couldn't believe it when Mimi called me and told me that she had heard that everything had been postponed until next week. So, I called Pruitt and he thinks there is a possibility of something Thursday, but I won't let my hopes rise too high because it sure does hurt when they fall.

Honey, I am so sorry that I didn't write you yesterday. I really feel like a heel, but I just knew that tomorrow I would be talking to you in person and you wouldn't have time to get the letter. Of course, there really wasn't much to write because I had talked with you.

Darling, they had Communion at church last night and I was glad that I went. Joyce Dowling came and sat with me and I appreciated that. I was sorry that church was a little late getting out and I was late getting to you. Could you see better at the new place? I thought from your signal that you could.

After leaving downtown, we rode by the Stone's. Bud wants to buy the trailer. He said he would get me some money as soon as possible and I told him $25.00. Guess that is all right. I heard you tell Don you would give it to him for that.

Darling, since I heard the news today, I have had such a let down feeling, I can hardly stand it. I can't think of a thing to write about. All I can think about is you and your being up there.

Honey, I just don't know what to do. I would give anything if I could just see you and talk with you today.

Had a wire from your Daddy last night. He said that there wasn't anything much wrong with the car and Cecil would take care of it.

Had a letter from Cecil today and he said if things worked out for you to call him and everything would be alright. Even the service time will be alright. The letter was very formal and written by his secretary. It said that he sincerely hoped everything would work out the way we wanted. He has discussed it with Mr. Sneed and he said he was sure they could work out something that would be satisfactory with you. The supervisors for Alabama and South Carolina will be in the office Wednesday and if things materialize, he is sure that something can be done so that your service record will not be broken.

I am writing him today explaining what has happened and that it may be later on in the week but that I will keep him posted.

Honey, I guess I had better write your Daddy, too, because he was very confident when he talked with Pruitt that it would all be over tomorrow.

The notices for the Southern Life Insurance came today but it isn't due until the 19th, so I will save it until the last.

I have tried to talk with the real estate man but haven't had any luck in reaching him today. I wish we could sell this house. I hate to even bother to clean it up. Honey, there just isn't any purpose in keeping house without you here to enjoy it.

Darling, I feel so lost and helpless without you. I hope that Pruitt went to talk with you today. His secretary promised that they would get word to you about what happened.

I'm so ashamed of myself. I'm so cross with everyone. I called the Flynns to tell them what has happened and Harry said, "Well, good. I believe the longer they wait, the better off Bob will be when his case comes up." And I hung up in his face. Later I called him back and said that I wouldn't be so upset at the postponement if you were out.

Honey, I love you with all my heart and wish I could do something for you. You are doing so wonderfully well and you have it much harder than I do. It makes me ashamed that I am so weak. But, if I could just be with you, I think I could survive.

I'll write you again tonight, but I wanted to get this in the mail. I love you, darling.

Yours,
Joyce

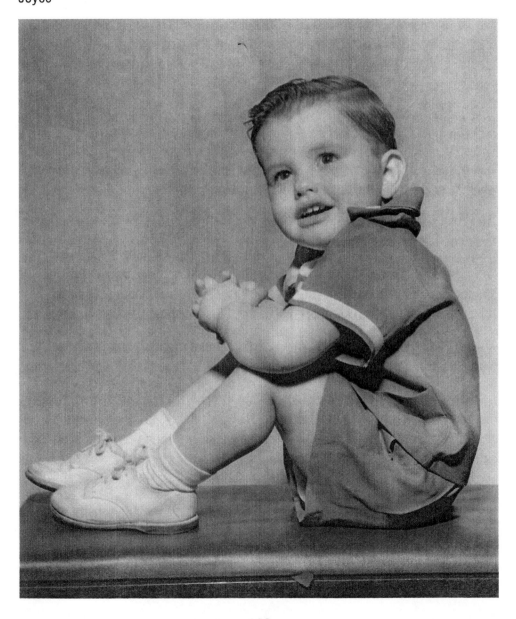

Monday Nite
December 5, 1955

Hello Sweetheart,

I'm a little worried. No doctor yet and it is after 7. I'm getting pretty shook up for fear something may be wrong.

You know I have been thinking. I'm sorry we contacted 7th Street *(Cutulo)* at all because someone may say the wrong thing.

This has been an awful rough day. I'm sure looking forward to 8:30.

Baby, I have just got to be with you for a while. I want you so much. I just need to hold you real close to me. I wish I knew something new to say but as you know, things are about the same every day here.

I sure hope that if this does go to Circuit Court, I'll be able to get out on bail a while.

It has been hot today and the food hasn't been too good. In fact, this is just a bad day.

Sweetheart, if it ever works out, I can just see those mountains up in the country calling us. It will be wonderful I'm sure. Keep you chin up and we will have happier days. Guess I'll close.

All my love to you and Ron.

Love,
Bob

Monday PM
December 5, 1955

My Dearest Darling,

Guess I am about at my lowest ebb tonight. Honey, I think each time something happens that I can't take much more but I manage to survive. It was a real heartbreaker to learn today that nothing would happen tomorrow. You know, darling, I kept trying not to get my hopes up but I just can't help it. But I know everything is going to work out all right eventually and we must not get impatient. I'm awfully impatient anyway and I can't see why this must drag on. I'm sure it must all be for the best.

Darling, I know you aren't going to like it but I am going to go to work tomorrow. Honey, someone has just got to do something. We keep spending when there is nothing coming in. Bill Culbreth came by for a few minutes today. They need a girl for a couple of weeks to do some extra work. I told him I wanted to be free to do whatever I could for you and he said he understood. I also said that when the trial came up I intended to be there and he said all right. So I guess it is about the best place I could work on a temporary basis. Honey, I went over to the Riverside Nursery to see about putting Ron in. They charge $10 a week. He has a hot meal at noon and they have beds for them to take a nap in the afternoon. I hate like everything to do it but I guess it is the best thing.

I took Ron to the doctor to get a health certificate. He said he needed a booster shot and also asked me if I wanted him to have the Salk vaccine for polio. So, I gave him both. I am supposed to take him back in a month for another Salk shot.

Darling, one of the shots was in his arm and one in his fanny. The one in the hip really seemed to bother him. He sorta limped around and couldn't sit down too good. And boy, if you sympathized with him he really got a hurt look on. I hope it will be all right in the morning. We sure did miss our Daddy!!

Honey, that is the reason I didn't bring Ron down tonight. He stayed with Mimi. But when I came back he wanted to see the big building so we rode back through town but I guess you couldn't see us.

I was so reluctant to leave tonight. I knew I couldn't do a thing but just stand down there and look up but it made me feel closer to you. I hope you can see me.

Pruitt's secretary told me this afternoon late that someone had gone up and told you the scoop. I sure hope she was telling the truth. I'm going to call Pruitt again first thing in the morning to be sure he is still working on it.

Darling, each day gets longer and longer. I can't even keep track of what day in the week it is. They all seem so unimportant except Sunday when I see you.

Honey, there was an article in tonight's paper about *(Judge)* Willard being sick. It told about Guy's trial being postponed and then it went on to say that his arrest coincided with yours. And went into detail again about you being picked up in Jacksonville – Willard ordering you examined, etc. Just the same stuff.

I guess you are thinking about Ron's birthday coming up Sunday. I hated to mention it but I know you are thinking about it anyway and I was wondering if you had anything special in mind that you would like for him to have. I really don't know but I didn't think I would spend much. I don't know what we will do about a party but we'll have something. I wish you could see him.

Honey, I guess I'm getting lazy but I sure do hate the thought of going to work in the morning. I'll have to get up at 6:00 to get to work by 8:30. But I'll get used to it. Honey, I feel that it is best since the job won't keep me from you and is temporary. After all, people have been good to us and we do have to help ourselves.

Tell Carl *(Cellmate)* hello. Is he taking good care of you?

Darling, I hate to close but I must. It is nearly midnight. Wish you were laying here beside me. Sure is lonesome by myself.

Honey, I love you with all my heart. Stay sweet as ever and hurry home.

All our love,
Joyce

Tuesday Nite
December 6, 1955

Hello Sweetheart,

Boy, what a day this has been. Ever since the one blink last night, I have been wondering what the trouble is. I haven't heard a word all day. So you can see I'm in quite a state tonight. I have made up my mind though that I will stop hoping for anything. And if anything happens someday, I'll just be pleasantly surprised. I just wish that I could be out for Ron's birthday or at least Christmas. However, honey, I want you to try your best to put my troubles out of your mind and go about making something of a normal life for you and Ron. You can't keep on living in hope and despair. So honey, use your best judgement in everything and we will just hope to someday pick up the threads. Just keep on remembering I love you more than life itself and that if I didn't, I wouldn't have any more troubles.

If you think it is best, go ahead and try to go to work. Unless Pruitt knows something about when I'll be getting out. If I were you, I would try Independent Life because I'm afraid anything else would not pay enough to live on and put Ron in a decent nursery school. I wish that Mamie Tyler could take care of him. Then we would know he was getting the best of everything.

Honey, if the letter seems a little down in the mouth, forgive me. However, I'm trying to get to a place where I have a little peace in my mind and the only way I know to do this is to sorta bury my thoughts in nothing.

I love you, my dear, and would give anything in this world to hold you close. God bless you and Ron.

Love,
Bob

P.S. Tell Pruitt if he gets time to come see me. Also ask him to try to bring you if he can. Maybe I can see you through the wire.

Tuesday
December 6, 1955

Hi my darling,

This is really one of those nights when I need you bad. Your letter was so sweet today. Darling, you are being mighty brave and wonderful and I'm sure you will be rewarded for it. I feel so helpless and would love to be able to help. But I am confident that it won't last much longer.

Sweetheart, this has really been a day. I went to work. Guess I must have been getting soft because I sure am beat tonight. The work really isn't hard. It is just the mental strain. You are on my mind so much. And, I was concerned about Ron and nursery school. However, he seemed to make out fine. He was delighted with everything and I know the woman real well who is his teacher.

Darling, everybody at First Baptist was mighty nice. The work is just more or less being general flunkie. It sorta kept me occupied and we can use the money.

We are doing fine because we know we have a bright future ahead when we can all be together as a family and even though we are separated we are still a family and we need you. Every day we talk about Daddy. Ron always has something he is going to get Daddy to fix.

Honey, about 4:30 this morning Ron came and got in bed with me and that finished my sleep. But I guess he was just lonesome and I enjoy having someone sleep close to me.

Tonight we went to the Flynn's for dinner. It was nice and I sure did appreciate it.

Did you see me with the binoculars? They didn't do the trick though. I could catch a glimpse of you just as you struck a match. Sorry we couldn't stay long but Ron was tired and I couldn't hold him long.

Darling, we got our first Christmas card today. It was from Nolan Brown Cadillac Company. They're wasting their money sending us a card. If they think we'll be buying a new Cadillac this year – I have news for them.

I had already talked with Guy when I got your letter. However, it had no effect. Things are too far along to change either. I hope and pray that things will work out differently next time.

It seems that there is so little to tell. I manage to keep busy but it sure isn't anything exciting.

Did I tell you that Dean, from the office, and the fellows he sings with won on Arthur Godfrey's program last week?

Sweetheart, we love you with all our heart. Someday we'll really start living again and I'll be the happiest person in the world.

Love you,
Joyce

Wednesday Noon
December 7, 1955

Hello Sweetheart,

I'm starting your letter a little early today. I just got the letter you wrote Monday.
I have been wondering all this time why I didn't go to court Tuesday. I was afraid
everything had gone wrong because I have never seen the doctor. However, I take
it that the reason for the delay is the judge's sickness. Looks to me like though, if
it is definitely going to his court, that he could set bail. I sure hate to be here on
Ron's birthday. Looks like I will though.

I'm glad you heard from Cecil and hope he will be able to hold out a little longer.
If Pruitt still thinks everything is OK, then I guess you might as well pay the credit
union the $148. However, use your own judgement. Also, I'm afraid I sounded
pretty down in the letter you got yesterday. If it looks good don't go to work unless
you want to.

Honey, get Ron a little car or something and tell him it is from his Daddy for his
birthday.

My darling, I think that my love for you builds up more and more each day and
though I look forward to maybe leaving Miami, the thought of having to leave you
here, even for a little while... that's why I hope the house will soon sell. I know it
is a burden for you to try to keep it up and I hate for you to have to worry about
anything else.

I think it is wonderful the way you are doing everything and I know Ron must upset
you some. But baby, hold on and be good to him because I'm sure that he is upset
too and I know the little fellow must know when something is wrong. I just wish I
could be there to put my arms around you and say everything is OK.

It's a good idea to sell the trailer to Bud. I will have to send him the ball off the
Hudson or he can get one at 36th St. & 27th Ave. at a trailer place. They are only
about $1.00.

I just got your Friday & Saturday letters. They really built me up. A letter from you is like a tonic to me.

Honey, I know that you are not discussing everything with anybody but I just wanted to say again that I especially wouldn't say anything else to 7th Street *(Cutulo)*.

Love,
Bob

Wednesday
December 7, 1955

My dearest Bob,

Well, another day is gone and we are a little closer toward being together once again. Honey, you just don't know how I ache to hold you in my arms. I feel so alone and lost without you. I need your love and I need you close to me. It is so heartbreaking that we should be so close and yet so far apart. But my heart and my love are with you always. You are ever in my thoughts and I really long for you.

Sweetheart, I could have cried when I got your letter written Monday and you hadn't heard anything. Pruitt promised me that you would be told. If he couldn't go he would send someone from his office.

I am enclosing a newspaper article that was in today which explains your situation pretty much. Of course, by now you probably know all of this. The first I knew was when I picked up the paper. So, it looks like you will be seeing two doctors instead of one.

Honey, I worked hard today. There was a good bit of mimeographing to do and I really kept busy.

Ron didn't take his "fawnfee" to school with him today. He said the teacher told him not to bring it. But the first thing he asked when I picked him up was if I had it in the car. He seems to like the school real well. Bud took Ron and Susan this morning and saved me a trip. I think he is going to take them tomorrow, too.

Darling, you know I told you I was having trouble with the brakes? Well, I went by Jack's this afternoon and he put some fluid in but said he wants me to come in Saturday so he can check to see if there is a leak in the master cylinder. I guess I better have it checked.

I left Ron with Mimi tonight. He was tired and didn't want to come. So I knew if I brought him down he would just give me a fit. Darling, I could see your outline tonight. I couldn't see your face but I knew it was you.

I sent a check to the credit union today because I had promised them I would take care of it this week. So we can breathe on that one for another month anyway. I hated to spend that much money but I thought we ought to. You know, darling, I was thinking about how many times you said, "I think I could spend the rest of my life in bed." So enjoy it because you are really going to have to work when it is over.

I feel like I keep repeating myself but there isn't much to write about. Mimi has been so good to us that I would really like to fix dinner for them on Ron's birthday but I hate to spend the money or the time right now.

I forgot to tell you that we're going to have to buy another pillow. Ron has decided he must sleep with a pillow.

Honey, guess I must try to get a little sleep. I'm thinking of you my darling and looking forward to that wonderful day when we will be together again.

I love you,
Joyce

Ron with Susan Stone

Thursday
December 8, 1955

Hello Sweetheart,

I just got your letter you wrote Monday night. So you can see I haven't had much news this week. If Pruitt has sent any word up here, I haven't heard about it and don't have any idea just what is going on. I have guessed that the hold up is on account of the judge being sick but, of course, I don't know whether it has been sent to his court or not. I wrote Pruitt a letter yesterday and asked him to come up but I don't know whether he will or not.

Honey, my heart nearly broke when I read about you going to work. It nearly kills me to be sitting here while you have to work and Ron is in nursery school. I can only pray that it will be for a short while.

I'm glad you took Ron to the doctor. I think it is good to have him have the polio shot.

I'm afraid I can't give you much help on anything for Ron's birthday. Just be sure Larry takes his picture.

Have you discussed with Pruitt or anyone the possibility of me getting to see you under more favorable conditions? Don't know that it would do any good but might.

Honey, you will have to forgive me not saying too much about Ron's birthday or Christmas as I just can't write about that subject. But I love to hear from you about it.

Sweetheart, it scares me to love like I love you and I constantly worry about you and Ron and want you to take care of yourselves. Be sure and get the the car brakes fixed.

By the way, how much are you making at the church? I have to keep track you know. You might try to hold out on me – Ha!

Was Mamie T. interested in keeping Ron for $10 a week?

4:00 PM

Just saw Dr. Gilbert today. He was pretty nice. Hope everything was OK. So I guess that things are still going through channels. Maybe Tuesday will be the day. At least I have some idea of what must be going on.

You know, honey, if it were not for the circumstances, there are a few good laughs now and then as we all have our good days and bad days. Usually when one guy is down another is up, so that helps.

Baby, I love you and want you to keep holding on. We will make it yet.

Love to you both,
Bob

Thursday
December 8, 1955

Hello my darling,

I'm going to wring that Bill Pruitt's neck. He promised me faithfully that someone would talk to you Monday. Then Tuesday, Mrs. Fay told me that someone had been to see you on Monday to tell you what the score is. Of course, they didn't bother to call me. I had to read it in the paper.

Honey, I don't want to discourage you but Pruitt isn't saying too much about the time element. These doctors will have to examine you, then turn in their reports, then there will be a hearing in the circuit court and they can turn it back to Willard. Pruitt is still very confident but he said he can't tell how long it will take. He said maybe next week. But darling, I'm afraid to get my hopes up again. The letdown is just terrific – as you know. Tuesday night I just thought I had reached bottom.

I guess by now you have my letter telling you that I am working. I talked with Earl about the insurance job and he said under the present circumstances he thought I would be better off to go to work for Bill until we know something. The work is easy. The hours are good and they are very understanding about the situation. Of course, the money isn't too good but I guess it is as good as I could expect for something temporary. Did I tell you it's $45.00? If I have to work for a while, and I'm not counting on it, I'll probably change jobs. But when I took this job the first of the week I thought it would only be for a couple of weeks.

Darling, I try not to worry or to plan. I'm just trying to live from day to day. I guess if it weren't for Ron I would let everything go but it isn't fair to him. I spend the early part of the evening before we go to town playing with him or reading to him. I try to fix some decent meals, too. Even though I don't care a thing about eating.

I'm just going to get Ron a couple of things for his birthday because I know the Flynns and Mother will give to him and I want to save some money for Christmas.

Baby, I'm going to try to get Ron's record payer this week because I'm afraid they will all be gone. I want to get something that he can play himself because that is half the fun.

I don't even like to think of Christmas but I just feel that the good Lord is going to see that we are together. Christmas has always been such a special time for us that I feel sure this year it will be extra special because it will mean a new beginning. You know darling, surely we have done enough good in our lives that the Lord will realize we can mean something to him if he will but give us the chance.

I've always thought that we got along better than most couples we know. Now, I am sure that we have something far deeper and more beautiful. I believe this experience has proved to us that we know a real love.

Sweetheart, I ache so to have you and to hold you. It has been so long since we have been together. It is actually three weeks today but it seems like a century. Little did we know it would drag out this long when we went down that day.

Darling, I have got to get my thoughts together about Ron's birthday but I just don't know what. I think I will buy a cake because it will be fancier than if I made it. I don't know what to get him because being in the nursery all day, he really doesn't need too much in the line of toys. Of course, he can always use clothes but that isn't very exciting. I think I will get him something inexpensive so he will have several packages to open. I would give anything to have you with us.

It is impossible for me to live a normal life without you and I refuse to even try. But I have to do something for Ron's sake. You know, what we do now may have an effect on his entire life and I want to be careful. I want him to feel secure and that he is loved and I'm just going to have to force myself to do some things that I don't feel like doing. I really don't feel like doing anything.

Honey, I too, wish that Mamie could keep Ron but when I told her I was going to work she didn't offer. Really, what little I could pay would hardly make it worth her while.

Sweetheart, just try to look toward the future when we will be together. You'll be wishing you didn't have to listen to my grumbling and eat broccoli and asparagus. Who knows, I may even put you on another diet!! But, I think you'll have to gain a little back before I do that.

We have a lot to be thankful for and a lot to look forward to. This isn't going to last forever. When we celebrate our silver wedding anniversary we'll look back on that ninth anniversary and wonder if it ever happened.

Darling, could you tell that Ron had on his pajamas tonight? He was really tired and I was, too, after I held him for a while. We couldn't see you but we did see the light and knew you were there.

All our love,
Joyce & Ron

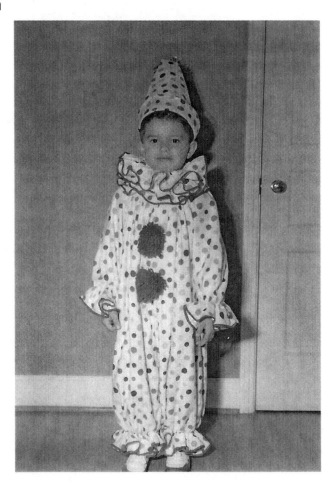

Friday
December 9, 1955

Hi Honey,

Almost another day made. I feel like this is a terrible waste of life just sitting and watching the sun come up and go down. I just don't think it will be this way always.

One of the lawyers from Pruitt's office came up today. I understand he was supposed to come last Monday and is just getting here today. It seems that I'm to see still another doctor. I think his name is Anderson. He is supposed to be a friend of Preacher. I understand Preacher is sick and that that is a source of some of this tie-up. Wish the guy would come on though, so this thing would get in one court or the other so I could get out on bond. I may be wrong but I sure don't understand this bond deal. I always heard that the only thing you couldn't get a bond for was murder. But I guess this will work out, too.

Honey, I guess Cecil has gotten tired of us writing him that the deal is over Tuesday and then Thursday and then some other day. I never heard of so many screwed up deals.

Say baby, I sure need you. You know what I mean. It has been a long time and I'm really ready. I'd just about give anything to get close to you again.

I hope your work isn't too hard. I feel so bad about you having to work all day and then come home and take care of Ron. I know it is a big strain. But every day I pray to God to give you the strength you need. Baby, take care of yourself and eat good and don't stand on the street at night and hold Ron too long. I had a backache last night just watching you holding him. My darling, you must take care of yourself because the only thing I have left on earth is you and Ron and oh, how I love you.

When I think of you having to do these things, I think the first bitterness that I have really felt creep into my heart about Betty & Buddy. I don't minimize my own faults and sins but honey, I hope some day they will be made to realize what they have done to add to our trouble. I hope I never have to see either one of them again, as I don't think I could take it.

I'm looking forward to seeing you Sunday, honey, but wish it didn't have to be through the glass.

Honey, look around the house and see if we have either a small Bible or New Testament and if we have one, see if they will let you bring it in.

I hope you get this letter Saturday. Anyhow, let me say this. Just 3 years ago Sunday nite about 6:30, you gave me and yourself about the most wonderful gift a man could ever have, our little boy. God was good to us then and will be again. My darling, I can never make it up to you for the terrible thing I have done to you and to the Lord but my darling, I'll certainly do everything in my power to make both of you happy the rest of our lives. I only hope the good Lord will let me start soon. Oh! How I love you.

Guess I'll close now and say goodnight. I'm sending Ron his birthday card.

Love to you both,
Bob

Friday
December 9, 1955

Hi Darling,

One more day to mark off our calendar. They surely do drag by, don't they, honey?
But in another way they really speed by.

When I got home tonight Ron was really dead tired. I just had to bathe him and get
him ready for bed. Well, he went to sleep and it was so cold that I hated to drag
him out. I was afraid he would catch cold. So, I talked myself out of going down.
I knew you would understand. But darling, when it got to be 8:30 my heart was
just breaking because, of course, you would have no way of knowing why I didn't
come. So I bundled Ron up and we got in the car. We parked by the nearest place
– thinking you would see us and I could still be close to the car. My heart nearly
broke when I could see you up there and you couldn't see me. I got out and stood
for a while–got back in the car and then got out again. Finally, I drove around to
the other place and stood there. I could have kicked myself for even thinking that I
could miss a night.

Darling, the preacher has been sick this week with the virus. They sent him out of
town. Of course, I believe they really are just telling people that so they will leave
him alone.

Ron seems to be having a big time in nursery school. He talks a lot about it. His
teacher's name is Mrs. Waterhouse and he is always telling me something about her.

I will get Ron something tomorrow for his Daddy to give him for his birthday.
Honey, I would give most anything if you could just be with us. But darling, at least
I can see you Sunday.

Believe it or not, Ron and I get along remarkably well. I guess it is another one
of those things that the Lord takes care of. Because I don't seem to be as short
tempered with him. I try to be sweeter and more loving. He is very affectionate.
But honey, he is too smart a little boy not to realize what is going on.

I hope you aren't freezing to death tonight. It sure is cold here.

I love you with all my heart. Keep sweet.

Love,
Joyce

Saturday
December 10, 1955

Hi Sweetheart,

Guess another day is about shot. I think Saturdays and Sundays are about the hardest. Just wonder if this is the last one I'll have to spend here. Spent most of the day in bed trying to keep warm. It is really cold up here. I thought today would have been a good day for us to ride around and do things. Hope you and Ron didn't freeze to death last night.

This will reach you Monday or Tuesday, I guess. If by that time the deal has been thrown back into Willard's court and he is still sick – I should be able to get bond. You might bring this up to Pruitt. The only thing that worries me is that I understand another doctor is supposed to see me and he hasn't come yet.

Honey, I know I must repeat myself many times but time is so confusing and I lay and think so much that I forget what I write and don't write.

I haven't gotten a letter from you since Monday. Guess I'll get them tomorrow. I sure enjoy your letters and read them many times.

Baby, I can't think of anything much to write tonight as I'll be seeing you tomorrow and all I can think of is that.

Sweetheart, I love you so much and really miss you – especially this time of the year it is hard to be apart as we always enjoy this time of year so much.

I just have a feeling that this week ought to bring something good. I certainly have been praying overtime.

Well, I'll close this and get it off. Remember my heart is with you every minute of the day and night. Take care of yourself and don't work too hard.

Love to you both,
Bob

Sunday
December 11, 1955

Hi Sweetheart,

Sunday is about gone and I'm sorta glad. This is always a long day. It is a long time until you get here and it is an even longer time after you leave.

Honey, you looked so pretty today. I don't remember when you have looked any better. I thought about you and Ron this afternoon about 3:00. I just wondered if you all were singing Happy Birthday.

That little fellow sure looked cute tonight. Boy, I would have jumped out just to feel his little arms around my neck. You are pretty lucky, you know, to have the privilege. Of course, I'd even swap that to be able to hug his mother.

I'm anxious to hear about the results of the party.

I'm so proud of the sweater. It is really beautiful. I don't think I want to wear it in this place unless it gets mighty cold. It is made to show off. You showed good taste in picking it out. But, then you have good taste in picking everything – look what you picked for a husband. Ha! Ha! Ha!

Carl *(cellmate)* says that if he gets out before I do, I had better look out as he thinks you are mighty pretty. He got a kick out of saying hello to you.

Honey, I know you mustn't spend too much money for a tree but try to get a fairly large one for Ron's sake. I want him to think that his tree is as big as anyone else. If Guy is out, he might get you one off the market. He is pretty good at that. Last year I got ours at Stephens but the Curb Market is good too.

Things sure change don't they? Here you are, doing everything. Thank God for a wife like you who can do.

Guess I'm all wrote out except that I love you so much. Thanks for being just you.

Love to you both,
Bob

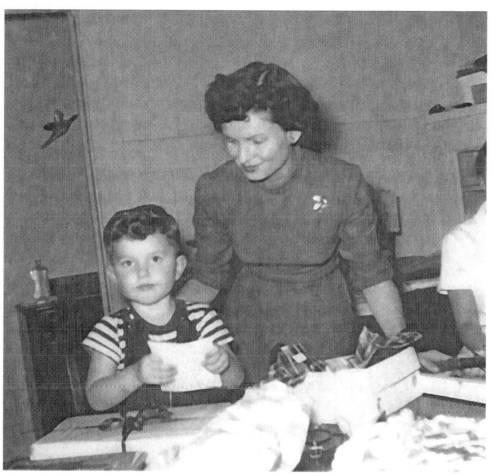

Joyce & Ron, December 11, 1955

Sunday
December 11, 1955

Hi Darling,

It was so wonderful to see you today. But I always hate it so bad when two o'clock comes and it is all over. Darling, you looked so good to me today. I didn't realize how good-looking you were. I hope you will take care of yourself and try to relax so that you can sleep some.

Honey, I know you are anxious to hear all about our "Happy Birthday." Well first, Mother had a birthday dinner for Ron. She had a pretty cake. She gave him a cute pair of brown dungarees lined with flannel and June gave him a tablet, crayons, balloons and bubble water. She said they sang Happy Birthday to him and then he sang Happy Birthday to them.

When I left you, I went to the store – called Mother and she said Ron was still awake. So I picked him up – got the cake and ice cream and went to Mimi's. Barbara, Eunice, Pottie, Pat, Little Harry & Mamie T. were all there. He really had a big time. His cake had yellow flowers on it and in blue said "Happy Birthday Ron." He even wanted to light the 3 candles. We all sang Happy Birthday and he blew them out. I could hardly sing for thinking about you.

Honey, the Flynns all gave him a bunch of stuff and their cards were all separate. As he looked at each card he wanted to give it back to the person who had signed it. They gave him a little metal train, ukulele, a plastic thing with a chicken on it that you pull a little string and they peck the dish. Mimi gave him an adorable suit. The pants are brown gabardine with the checked cuff. It is a 4 and fits him just right.

Mamie T. gave him a xylophone which he loves. Honey, I think I told you that I got him a little white furry kitten and put your name on it. I was so glad I picked that because he loves it and tells everyone his Daddy sent it to him. I also put your name on the Davy Crockett bedroom slippers. They are cute and have fur on them. I gave him a puzzle and a ukulele that plays Davy Crockett.

Ron hugged everybody and gave me a kiss on the back of the neck. He was so excited he could hardly eat but he served everyone else.

Pottie had had a couple of beers and was really wound up. She played Ron's ukulele and sang.

Oh – even Pat gave Ron a little tiny dog.

Then Ron wanted to help Harry wash his car, so we stayed a while longer.

Brownie called and said he had been to a big fire down Flagler Street and was soaked and wanted some dry clothes. So Ron went with Harry to take them.

Honey, Ron didn't get a nap so he was tired when we came to see you. I hope you could see him because he looked adorable.

We took some pictures, honey, but Larry didn't come. However, I am going to get him to take a picture of him all dressed up.

Darling, Ron kept talking about his kitten and saying, "When is my old Daddy coming home?" until I thought I couldn't stand it.

Mother kept Ron and I went to church. Honey, I went out to First Church because it was too late to get to Central. I saw the DeBordes and they just hugged me and she invited me to come eat lunch. They asked how you were and said to send you their love. I am so thankful that we have Christian, real Christian, friends. They are just wonderful.

Then, I went back for Ron. He was asleep and like a ton of bricks. Honey, he is such a sweetheart. I'm ashamed when I leave him for a little while.

Mimi said that Addie *(Cutulo)* had tried to call me but I haven't talked with her. I will, though, but not tell her anything about our situation.

It was so wonderful to see you today. I'm praying that I won't have to wait until next Sunday to see you. This week may see the end of things.

Sweetie, you know today we were talking about going to the seminary? I'm going to pray continuously about it and you do the same. I want us to do the Lord's will – whatever it is and I think we are ready. I believe our hearts are open so we can hear him talking.

This letter is terrible but I'm about to go to sleep.

Be sweet, my dearest. Know that we love you and are anxiously waiting for everything to be over.

All our love, always.
Joyce and Ron

Ron, December 11, 1955

My dad's letter to my mother, on December 12th, finds him hoping for a Circuit Court hearing on Thursday, with his case going to Criminal Court the following Tuesday. He says: "I know that this is doing some wishful thinking but if I should get out next Tuesday, I wish I could stay through Christmas and fly to Jacksonville about mid-afternoon and then drive on to wherever I'm going. It all depends on what the circumstances are."

He concludes with: "Baby, I hear the tales here about some of these guys and their wives and their way of getting along. Honey, I realize more and more every day what a wonderful marriage we have had. It just makes me love you that much more. My darling, it is hard for me to understand how a man could foul up when he has the kind of wife I have."

On December 12th my mother wrote that she gave Mimi $10 to pay for the anniversary gift my father had her purchase. There was a little left over that she wanted her to keep toward the film used and food. She went on to say that Mimi was "tickled to get" a letter from my dad. And she continued with telling him she had gone to town to shop for Christmas but hadn't accomplished a thing. However, she planned to go on Saturday to look for a record player for me.

She addressed my dad's earlier comment regarding Betty and Buddy with: "Honey, I read what you said about Betty and Buddy and I can see why you feel the way you do. But the Bible tells that we must not judge people and so regardless of what they have done to hurt us, I try not to judge them. It hurts mighty bad but I have to live with myself and it would be a lot harder to live if I had hate in my heart. Darling, they will be the ones to suffer in the long run because they harbor that feeling of hate. This experience and these horrible days will pass away and the love that we have will make us far happier that they can ever hope to be feeling as they do."

My mother went on to say: "Darling, the things you said about Ron being born to us were just beautiful. It makes me ashamed of some of the things I have felt in my heart. You know honey, when all of this started, I questioned why in this wide world the Lord would give us a child and then let this happen. I wasn't concerned about us, but about Ron. How unfair it was to bring him into the world. But, many times I have thanked the Lord for him because particularly since you have been up there, Ron has been my world.

He has been so understanding and good that I can't believe he is ours. I pray every day that the Lord will make me a good mother and help me to lead Ron in the right way."

She concluded with: " Baby, when all of this is over, we ought to really be able to write a love story, because I don't believe anyone could love deeper or greater than we do."

Tuesday
December 13, 1955

Hi Darling,

You know I get so aggravated when I think about having to write you when you are
so close. If I could just see you every day or talk with you on the phone. Honey, all
day long I think of things I want to tell you and when I sit down to write, I forget
part of them.

Sweetheart, every thing is going to work out. Everyone seems very encouraging. The
preacher is still talking. I'm just praying that things will hurry up and come to a climax.

Kap called this morning. He was so tickled with your letter. I explained things as
best as I could. He said he loved you like a brother. He wanted to know why we
couldn't get you out. Also, he asked me if I needed any money. He said to be sure
and keep him posted. I told him I would call as soon as I knew something. He said
he was going to try to go to see you.

Honey, I called Addie to find our their situation. Their deal won't come up until after
the first of the year. The calendar was full this week and next week their witnesses
will be out of town. They were pretty depressed. But I told them how lucky they
were. I could wait six months for yours to come up if you could just be out.

Darling, I didn't tell Addie *(Cutulo)* anything about your situation, so don't worry.

I took Ron to get a hair cut *(Guy Cutulo's older brother, Vincent, was our barber)*
tonight and then we ate at the store so we could get downtown in time. The food
was horrible. We had a pork chop with dressing and it was so greasy!!

We came on home early tonight and I put Ron to bed. Darling, every night when he
says his prayers he prays, "Bring my Daddy home soon."

The boy has been giving me a fit. Every time I do something he doesn't like he
says, "I'm going to tell my Daddy."

It's funny that you should mention about the Christmas tree in the letter I got today. I am enclosing a cartoon that was in this morning's paper. It was so like you that I just couldn't resist.

We'll get a big tree since we already have the decorations. Where do you think we ought to put it in the house? I think maybe where the record cabinet is or the television.

Darling, you had better wear that sweater. It will wash. In fact, you can wash it if you need to because it dries real fast. Does it fit?

Tell Carl I am mighty tickled with his flattery. He looks like a swell guy and I am glad you have him. I appreciate him because I know how much it means to you to have someone like him. But tell him I'm mighty jealous because he can be with you and I can't. Does he talk in his sleep and wake you up?

Did I tell you I got my check yesterday? $57.00... Boy, it sure does look big and it will help.

Darling, this new drive-in down the street has opened. I haven't had the heart to go down there because we talked about trying it out together.

I wish you could hear Ron say "Periwinkle." You know, that is the name of June's dog.

Sweetheart, this is one of those nights that I sure wish you were home. But, every night is like that. Some nights are just worse. Guess I will have to put out a red light and see if I can drum up some business. Ha! Ha!

Don't worry, as you always say – after having you I couldn't be satisfied with anyone else. And I know it is the truth.

I love you with all my heart. I'm so proud of the way you are holding up. Stay strong because it won't be much longer.

Good night, my darling. Keep sweet.

Love,
Joyce

"As usual I see your eyes were bigger than our living room."

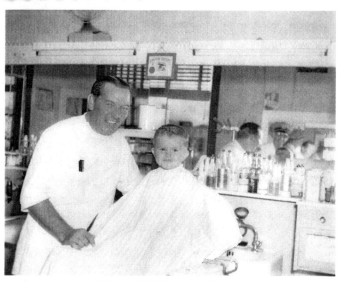

Ron with Vincent Cutulo

Tuesday
December 13, 1955

Hello Sweetheart,

Well, 'bout got another day licked up here. Sure enjoyed my two pieces of bread
and cup of tea that I had tonight. They had minced ham on it and you know that is
my one big pet peeve in meats.

Was glad to get word today about things. I sure hope if the Circuit Court sends it
back and I will then be able to get bond or something. So if everything goes so that
I have to leave immediately, I might have a few days in between with you and Ron.
vHoney, if you feel so inclined, I'd sorta like to have a little miniature chess set.
One of the fellows here knows how to play and says that he will teach me. If they
cost more than $1.50, don't bother as I couldn't enjoy it if it cost very much. I
don't know whether they would let you bring it up before Sunday or not. You
would have to call Chief Sims up here for permission. Now if Pruitt thinks I might
have a chance to get out this week then don't bother with it. If it works out though,
we will call it my Christmas present.

Honey, I have another thing to ask you to do. Carl wrote his mother about three
weeks ago and hasn't heard a word from her. He would like to have you call her
collect for him. Ask if she got his letter and if she is alright and if she is going to be
able to send him any money. Try to find out one way or the other whether she is or
not. He is so worried that he hasn't heard and also his lawyer won't do anything
until he gets some money.

Boy, I'm sure giving you the orders tonight just like you didn't already have your
hands full. I understand somebody else has you calling the V.F.W.

You know honey, I'm the only one up with a wife that can do something and all
the fellows seem to be interested in our doings. I really enjoy telling them about
my wife. And that is easy because I have the most wonderful one in the world.

I'm wondering tonight how Guy came out. It will probably be Sunday before I
know. I sure hope he is able to make out.

Saw you going to town last night. I'll bet you were tired. I kinda kept a lookout to see you go home. We worked it in relays.

Love,
Bob

Wednesday
December 14, 1955

Hi Darling,

It is nearly 11:30 PM and I am just starting your letter. So, if it doesn't make good sense, please forgive me.

Honey, I am delighted that Pruitt sent someone up to tell you what the situation is now. They told me that they would, but you know I can't count on them. I know you were probably disappointed that nothing would happen tomorrow, but it will all work out. I just know next week will see an end to all of this.

Darling, Mother said that Carl called and said something about a long distance phone call. I guess I will get a letter explaining it and I understand that he has made it. Anyway, let me know if I can do anything.

This has been miserable weather lately. I got up early this morning and washed some clothes and hung part of them in the garage but part of them I hung on the line and of course they didn't get dry. My hair is all stringy and looks horrible.

I am enjoying my work. The girl I work with is wonderful. She has been so nice to me and really makes me feel right at home.

Bill is nice, too. He is quite a character. Of course, I can't help comparing him to Dr. Angell and of course, there is no comparison.

Honey, Mother picked Ron up from school and was going to keep him for a while tonight so I could come home and do a few things. Well, about time for her to get Ron, Barbara called and said they were going to put up the Christmas tree at the Flynn's tonight and wanted Ron to help. So, I let him go over there. You should have seen him rushing around handing things and holding things for them. They have a big tree and then they have a couple of little trees about a foot high that they were going to use on a table or something. Ron took one look and said, "Oh dear, what am I going to do with these many Christmas trees?" He finally decorated the little trees and he thinks they are his own personal property. I left and went to

prayer meeting at First Church for a while and when I came back he was still going strong and wasn't interested in going home at all.

Ron's latest expression is to say something and then say, "Ha! Ha!" I get quite a kick out of him.

Darling, I thought I would get a Christmas tree this weekend and Ron and I would decorate it either Saturday or Sunday. He wanted to know when he was going to have a tree at his home.

I wish I could find a home for this poor old dog. I know she must get lonesome around here because all I do is feed her and sometimes it is late at night when she gets that. But, on the other hand, it is a comfort to have her because I know she will bark if anyone should come.

Did I tell you that Mrs. Culbreth, the mother, has leukemia or cancer? The boys are pretty upset. Bill is going home next week to see her.

Honey, I sent in our Homestead Exemption thing. Guess it will be alright.

We got a telephone bill today for $13.95. It had some long distance calls on it... the one I made to Cecil when you were in Jacksonville, and the time you called me from Cocoa and then there is another call to Jacksonville. Guess we called Cecil again.

If I don't stay long at night, you understand. I always feel that you think I am rushing off some place and you have to stay up there. But, honey, there is nothing I can do but wave. If there were, I would stay there all night. You know that.

I hope the radio and TV are fixed. I know that it helps to pass the time away some.

Darling, your hopes for next week sound wonderful. However, I just can't let myself plan because it hurts too bad if they don't work out. But honey, some way we are going to be together for Christmas. You know, darling, this may sound crazy, but I sorta wonder since you have served so much time already that maybe the judge will just let you go and you will be free to do what you want. Then you could stay through Christmas and leave and go to work on Monday. But we will

work it out some way because I don't think I could stand it without you. It would be wonderful if we could be together here in Miami. But, if we can't, we will work out something.

Sweetheart, you were talking about the other fellows and their wives. You know, it is hard for me to understand why a wife wouldn't be up there trying to see her husband and helping him. I can't see how they could have loved them much in the first place if they can't stick by them when the going gets rough. It makes me feel bad when I know how those fellows feel and I just wish I could do something for them.

I went to Jefferson's today to look at record players. They had a plastic one for $8.88 and then the next one was $18.00. I think I can do better than that. Ron has learned that you are supposed to ask Santa Claus for things so everything he sees he says he wants Santa Claus to buy that for him.

It seems like it has been an eternity since we have been together. You write so much flattery in your letters that I am going to be spoiled. Besides, darling, you think I am better than I am because you haven't been with me in so long. You will have to get used to living with me again and realize that I'm a pure stinker and hard to get along with.

But, baby, I love you with all my heart and I know that I have lots of faults but I promise to try harder to be sweet and patient.

Darling, I'm looking forward to holding you in my arms again real soon.

All my love,
Joyce

P.S. Honey, Willard has sent all the cases like yours – whether they plead guilty or not – to the Circuit Court. They are all to be examined by psychiatrists. No one knows much more about it than that. Dan, the lawyer, is trying to find out when it will be done but they haven't picked them up yet. Don't know whether that is good or bad. I'm just thankful that yours is close to being over. Love you.

Wednesday
December 14, 1955

Hello Sweetheart,

How is everything out there in the big wide beautiful world? I haven't heard a thing today. Guess maybe I'll hear something tomorrow. You might tell Pruitt that, if he can, to try to wind up my deal before the 7th Street *(Cutulo)* trial comes up, as that is next week and won't help me at all.

Honey, I have talked about you and Ron all day and I'm sure that the fellows are getting tired of it. But it means a lot to me just to call your name.

You know, if it doesn't work out that the Independent can use me, I have another idea. And it is just an idea that I want to discuss with you. You know I'm concerned that I haven't done something down the line that the Lord wanted me to do. I don't know exactly whether it is music or something else. Maybe it is just to do more layman work. I'm just a little confused but I've been doing a lot of praying and I wonder if God has another plan for me that is for us. I want so much to talk it over with you and would like to talk to Dr. Angell. I've never felt just this way and I sure need some advise. Be thinking about it and the Lord willing, maybe we will get a chance before long to stand face to face and talk about it.

My darling, the days are long and the nights are longer without you. I hope to get some mail from you by tomorrow. I wonder if anyone can know how much I want to be with you and my boy.

I was just thinking about Daddy. I don't think he ought to come down as I'm afraid it might be too much for you. You use your own judgement. Unless I do get out soon, I couldn't get to see him anyway.

Guess I'll close and try to dream about you and Ron. Be sweet. I love you.

Bob

Wednesday
December 14, 1955

Hello Sweetheart,

I got two letters from you today. The ones you wrote Sunday and Monday. I also got a letter from Harry Flynn.

Sounds like Ron had a wonderful party Sunday. I know he had fun.

Last night I wrote you about calling Carl's mother. However, today he got to call her and then called your mother to tell you not to call. Guess you got the message.

The fellow, Fields, wants you to go ahead and get his things. If you can get them by Friday, he will owe $14.00. I think it's a good gamble and we couldn't lose on the deal, I don't think. I believe by the indication of your letter that Brownie worked last Sunday. If he did, that should put him off Friday and I'm sure he would help you. He could either meet you there at noon or when you get off and as soon as you get it set up, he could get the stuff and you could go on. Whatever way you think best. I guess you could put the stuff in the back bedroom closet. Enclosed is a note from Fields giving you an idea of what he has.

One of the men from Pruitt's office was up today and said that the reports should be in today or tomorrow. He says that as soon as it hits the other court, I should get bond. I'm afraid to get my hopes up but it might mean release this weekend.

Carl had some terrific news when he called his mother today. It seems his wife had twins. A boy and girl. He hasn't seen her in about 7 months and didn't know she was pregnant. He is pretty shook up about it.

We got the TV back today. It helps a lot to have it and also I need it to tell time.

Honey, you looked so cute down there tonight throwing kisses. I'll be so glad when I can get those at a shorter range. Baby, I sure love you and want you so bad. I feel like I have about half of me alive without you and my boy.

I sure wish that when I leave here you could go with me right then. I just hate to think of us even being parted again if we can just get together again.

Guess that's all except I love you. I love you.

Bob

Thursday
December 15, 1955

Hi Sweetheart,

Well, it has been four weeks today and it seems like a year. Darling, surely it won't go on much longer.

Before I go any further, the preacher called me today and everything looks wonderful. He is going to try to get up to see you tomorrow. Said he would have gone sooner but was afraid it might be embarrassing for you. Of course, he had no idea that it would be this long.

I guess you saw me going to town tonight. I didn't think I was going make it because Ron wouldn't walk at first. But we got the chess game, if I can just get it up to you. Ron was real thrilled with all the lights in Burdines *(Department store)* and the decorations. I didn't take him up to see Santa Claus because I'm still hoping we will be together next week and can take him.

Darling, I sure do hate to see it turn cold again. I know you will nearly freeze up there. You ought to have those pajamas you took to Gainesville last year to wear under your pants.

The other day Bill Culbreth took some slides of the office staff. He got them today and they came out pretty good. There is some new film that you can buy and you get it back in a hurry.

I don't know what I will do with Ron next week because Susan *(Stone)* doesn't go to school and he'll probably have a fit. The half-day pupils are off two weeks for Christmas vacation.

Honey, every day Ron comes home with pretty pictures he has colored. They try to teach him to color in the lines and sometimes he does pretty good.

I hope I got the message straight that Carl got to call his mother himself. I haven't

called but would be glad to if he hasn't already got in touch with her.

I knew you would be watching for me to come back from town tonight. It was good to know that you were.

Darling, we got our city tax notice today for $5.79. Thank goodness it isn't bad.

There seems to be no news from 7th Street *(Cutulo)*. They aren't sure what happens next.

Sweetheart, when it gets close to Sunday, I get so impatient. I can hardly wait to see you. I'm praying this will be the last Sunday.

I wish I had more to write but I feel very encouraged about everything. Keep sweet as ever. Tell Carl hello and give all the fellows my love.

I love you with all that is with in me. You are everything to me.

Yours forever,
Joyce

It continued to be a mystery why my dad's case kept getting postponed. Other than the judge being sick at one point, there was never another excuse given. Each week was a promise of a hearing that did not take place until eight weeks after the arrest. He had missed being with his family for Thanksgiving, his ninth wedding anniversary, and his son's third birthday. And now, he was hoping desperately to get out for Christmas.

On December 16th, my dad was thrilled to receive several letters, and referred to them as being "newsy" and "just like a big cool drink" to him. He had been feeling down, and explained the reason: "You see, when the fellow from Pruitt's office was here, he told me that they were to have a hearing Thursday and that I would get bond right after that. Well, Thursday afternoon passed and then all day today. I just couldn't imagine what had happened. I have been afraid that something else has gone wrong. However, from your letter dated Wednesday, I gather someone must have told you that nothing would happen Thursday. I don't understand what is going on. I just hope it is for the best as I haven't heard anything else yet. Guess I'll know something Sunday when you get here."

My mother's letter on the following day explained the fate of the chess set she bought for him: "Honey, guess you wonder why I didn't try to get the chess game up to you. Well, I did. Bill called someone that he knew and they said that about a month ago they ruled out letting them have chess. It seems some man drilled holes in the bottom of the men and put notes in them. Isn't that something? So, consequently, that is out. I sure am sorry because it would have been nice for you to learn."

She went on to express her concern for my dad's cellmate, Carl: "Honey, I know Carl must be pretty upset by his news. I guess she didn't tell him so that he wouldn't worry. I don't know how she kept a secret that long. I know he sure would like to see those twins. You know, honey, as bad as our troubles are, there are people worse off than we are."

On that same day, December 17th, my father wrote professing his love with an apology, saying: "I wish that I had a wide vocabulary so that I could write a real expression of the way I feel about you. But as you have told me, I'm pretty poor about saying those kinds of things. But honey, I have sat up here and I have had lots of time to think. I cannot think of a thing in this world that would be fun without you. I don't know as I look back how I could have gone off and left you like I did so many times. Everything I think about these days, I think in terms of can Joyce do this with me. Baby, we are going to be closer than we have ever been before. In short, I love you."

Sunday
December 18, 1955

Hi Sweetheart,

Boy you sure did look pretty today. The fellows here have elected you "Queen of Cell 2." I'm so proud of you, honey. Several of the fellows said today that you sure are pretty.

Honey, I hope that the house insurance is straightened out. We didn't talk about it too much. If State Farm can't get it straight, I think maybe Pat can get it for us for one year. It might be a little higher. Earl might be about to help you out if you have any trouble. Also, the car insurance – you said the notice came. Doesn't that have a due date some time in January?

Gosh, I hated to see the visiting hours end. It seems twice as lonesome as it did before you came. I know that this will be a long week waiting for something happen. I just hope something will happen.

The books you brought are fine and I certainly enjoy having the paper.

Wasn't that bird standing next to me a jerk? He has a hard way to go up here because he seems to think he is the only one up here. Hasn't any consideration for anyone.

Honey, I'm afraid I don't have much to say tonight as we talked out this afternoon – except to say, I love you baby with all my heart and pray to soon be with you and Ron.

Love,
Bob

Queen of Cell 2

Sunday 11:00 PM
December 18, 1955

Hi Darling,

I had thought I would get this letter started earlier so I would be thinking a little clearer and could remember more things to tell you.

It was so good to see you today. But it sure is a let down after I leave. However I feel confident that this week we will be together. It just has to be.

Please keep up your spirits because everything is going to work out alright.

After leaving you, I rode back by the store. Mimi and Harry were anxious to know how you were doing. They want so bad to be able to help you. Mimi asked me to take her home. So I sat around there for a few minutes. It really looks like Christmas at the Flynn's. The tree was beautiful the first day but it is sorta lopsided now – like it is about to fall on its face. The coffee table, dining room table and a card table are all loaded with presents, wrappings and cards. The house is a mess but it sorta gets you in the Christmas spirit.

Brownie had run an ad in the paper today to sell his boat and he had several calls. While I was there, some man was looking at just the boat and another man called wanting to buy the trailer & motor. So if he can get them together, he will have it made. It seems he is rather desperate for money. The fellow that loaned them money for the plane is sorta pushing him. I sure hope he can sell it.

Honey, Bobbie Stewart called and wanted to know how you were doing. She said they had a nice Christmas party Saturday night. They did have it at the office and had Bo's do the catering. They decorated the office real pretty with red and green tablecloths, holly, etc. She said that Dean and his group sang, some girl played the accordion and U.L. gave a speech.

Just as I got Ron in bed for his nap, someone came to look at the house. Ron never did go to sleep, so I finally let him get up and dressed and went down to see you. Then, we went to Royal Castle and got a hamburger and went on to church.

We came out to First Church because they were having their music program and the choir director was so excited. I know that he would like for the staff to hear it.

Darling, I took Ron in church with me and he was very good. I sat on the back row but he didn't let out a peep. *(Preacher)* Bill baptized and that upset Ron a little because the people were getting all wet and he didn't see how that man was going to get down.

When we were waiting to go in, Mr. DeBorde was standing outside and he stood Ron up on the rail that goes around the porch of the church. Ron said, "You better hold me. I might fall down and my Mommie wouldn't have any little boy."

Once during the music program some woman was singing a rather screeching song and Ron put his hands over his ears and whispered, "That lady sings too loud."

When we left church, Ron said he wanted to eat dinner, so we went to Howard Johnson's in the Springs and I got an order of fried clams and Ron ate practically all of them.

Darling, tonight when we went down to see you, Ron said, "My Daddy better come home. I'm tired of waving."

When I got home tonight, Kat called and said that Bud didn't have to go to the debit *(Work)* in the morning and would take Ron to school. Susan isn't going to school for the next two weeks, so I hope Ron will be happy to go without her. Honey, the morning school takes a regular Christmas vacation like the regular schools.

I can hardly wait until tomorrow afternoon to find out when we can get you out. I hope and pray that it will be Tuesday, but I'm afraid to get my hopes up.

Honey, I guess I had better close so I can get this in the mail. I love you with all my heart. It was so good to see you today.

Keep sweet and remember that we are doing everything we can. Keep praying and everything will work out alright.

All my love, forever,
Joyce

U.L. & Bobbie Stewart

Monday
December 19, 1955

Hi Sweetheart,

It's just about noon but I thought I'd start my letter anyhow as I thought of a thing
or two I wanted to ask you about.

Are you trying to send any Christmas cards or do you think that it is worthwhile to
try to get them out? I was just thinking that we usually send so many that it might
cost too much or I imagine that you wouldn't have time to get them out. Maybe if
you think so and it isn't too late, you might send cards to very close friends.

Also, did you try to send George Culver *(Cousin)* anything this year? What do
you think? I don't think it is absolutely necessary as we rarely hear from them.
However, whatever you think.

Knowing what is supposed to go on about this time today sorta has me jumpy. I
just wish I had some way of knowing what the decision is this afternoon. I'm afraid
though that Pruitt would never think to come up and tell me.

Looks like it is a beautiful day outside. I'd sure like to feel a little of that sunshine.

Say, I found a Psalm in the little Testament you sent me that seems pretty good to
me – try reading the 51st Psalm. That sure is a nice little Testament and I'm going
to make it a part of my personal equipment.

The old TV sure is full of Christmas, isn't it? It is good in a way and in a way, it is
pretty rough.

6:00 PM
Hi again. We just had supper. This has been one of those days. We would be
ashamed to give stuff like this to our dog. I'm just sitting here looking forward to
7 o'clock. Oh, honey, I pray this thing ends this week.

I gathered that you shook your head no indicating you had heard nothing or else nothing had happened. Try to get Pruitt to come up and see me and tell me something if you can get him to. If it looks at all promising, blink your lights once.

Of course, I'm disappointed but I'll keep hoping until Thursday anyhow.

I wonder if you know how much I would have liked to jump down there to you and hold you and Ron in my arms. Oh darling, I love you and want you so.

Guess I'll close. I love you,
Bob

P.S. Tell Dr. Angell, if he can, to try to come to see me.

Monday
December 19, 1955

Hi Darling,

How do you like this combination – red & green? The red pen and green paper was all I could find.

Honey, I wonder sometimes if you can read these letters when you get them. I'm sitting propped up in bed now. So I wouldn't be insulted if you told me to write a little plainer.

Darling, this has been quite a day. I talked with Mr. Pruitt around 2:00 this afternoon. He said there had been a hearing at noon today with Judge Gordon, the state attorney and himself. And they decided after reviewing the doctors' reports that they would send it back to Willard's court. So they went through whatever procedure was to have it on the docket for Tuesday morning. For a couple of hours I was really walking on air. Then around 4:00 PM, Mrs. Fay called back and said it had been called off and they are trying for Thursday. I told Pruitt to do everything possible but to have you out this week. He said he was really pushing it.

I almost hated to even go down there tonight because I knew you would be hoping for some news.

Sweetheart, it looks like when it rains, it pours. Mr. Lipscomb called this morning and said our insurance policy was cancelled. I asked him why and he said they didn't have to give an explanation. So I asked him for a suggestion and he had none to offer.

I called Earl and he suggested I call Neil Coates. So Neil is going to put a binder on it so he can get that off to the company and they will be satisfied. He said as an estimate it would probably cost round $106.00. I wasn't sure just how much insurance we had to have. But I have found our policy from State Farm so I can go by that. We will get a rebate on the other policy so there won't be too much difference.

I think I wrote you last night that a couple had come by to look at the house. Well, they came back today and offered us $2,000.00 over the mortgage. Which they considered as around $3,000.00 because they said for us to take it off the market and save that much. I told them I would have to talk with you and think about it. I just don't see how we can take that little.

Honey, I know we can never make enough to pay off all of our debts but if we could pay off a few, it sure would help. We have to consider that you won't be making as much as you have before and we can't make that many payments... besides, what we owe Raby, Kap and Pruitt. It is sure going to take a while to pay things off.

We went by Mimi's after work and she insisted that we stay and eat. There wasn't anyone but Brownie, Mimi, Ron and I. We had hot dogs.

Honey, Brownie is still trying to sell his boat. Several seem interested. He said today a man called and sounded really interested but couldn't come see it. So, Brownie hauls the boat way up on the Boulevard some place. When he gets there, he finds out it is the former owner of the boat and he just wondered how it looked.

Brownie is giving Elaine a portable radio for Christmas and she is really disappointed because she wants a diamond ring.

I didn't get the Christmas tree tonight because Ron was tired and I thought he needed to go to bed early. He didn't have a nap yesterday and didn't get to bed until late. So I guess we'll try tomorrow.

Darling, I wrote your Daddy today and also Cecil. I was so overjoyed when I thought something would happen tomorrow that I typed them each a note. The postman had already picked them up when I got the news that nothing would happen. So I guess I'll write them again tomorrow.

I wrote my sister Bobbye and briefly explained the situation. A girlfriend of hers is going up this weekend and Mother said she knew she would tell her. But Mother, not knowing I had written called her tonight. She said Bobbye was very sweet and wanted to know if she could do anything. I guess it is just as well that she knows.

Darling, it is nearly 12:30 AM and I have another busy day ahead. I am enjoying my work.

Your letter today was so sweet talking about us being together. You'll get tired of me tagging around before long but you know you'll have a hard time getting rid of me. I, too, am looking forward to us doing things together. You know, darling, this is the longest we have ever been separated and I don't like it.

Honey, in case you didn't know, we have about the sweetest little boy in all the world.

We are anxious to have you home.

All our love,
Joyce & Ron

Bob, Joyce & Ron with Bobbye Broadway Fortner

Tuesday 8:00 PM
December 20, 1955

My dearest darling,

Here it is... only 8:00 PM and I am settled down to write you. But, there is a good reason. Ron is spending the night with Mimi. We ate supper over there and she wanted him to stay. She said she wasn't going to work tomorrow and would keep him all day. I am delighted because it gives me a little time tonight and also it will be a change for him tomorrow.

Honey, Ron looked so cute today. He wore that yellow shirt that is trimmed in brown and his long brown pants and brown corduroy jacket. Bud took him to school today for me. Ron seems crazy about Bud and I think it is because he misses his Daddy so much. You know, honey, this experience makes me admire more people like Addie, Mrs. Hale etc. who have had to raise boys by themselves. These few weeks have been enough for me.

Darling, I've got the insurance all straightened out with Neil Coates. I don't remember the figure exactly but it will cost $97 and some cents. He said he would notify Independent for me and I could wait to send him the money until I get the check back from State Farm. We should have taken it out with him in the first place. He gave us the same coverage we had.

This has really been a long day. I waited all day to hear from Pruitt and finally called around 4 o'clock. He said it would probably go to court Thursday. So I blinked the lights tonight. I just hope we won't be disappointed.

I mailed the package to your folks today. Sure hope it gets there in time.

You know, I have been surprised that we have gotten as many Christmas cards as we have. Honey, Skipper Norris sent a beautiful card and wrote on the bottom "Thank you for the fun you gave me in scouting. If I can ever repay you, let me know."

Darling, Barbara got the record player for Ron, so I guess we're all set for Christmas except for a few little things. Guess I will have to get the tree tomorrow.

I made the payment on the rugs. The piano payment isn't due until the second of January. The car insurance is due Dec. 26. I have checked up on everything, so don't worry.

Hildreth called me tonight just to see how I was doing. They are sorta irked with U.L. because he won't let them take their vacation at Christmas. Earl is letting his men take theirs.

Honey, I have tried to ease up on my talking with Bobbie Stewart. She has been mighty good but every time she calls she sorta tries to pick me and I know she talks to several people. She called tonight and said she was going to bake me a cake.

June just came by. She said Bobbye *(Youngest sister)* had called tonight. She said she was crying and very upset. She wanted to know if I needed any money. June was very nice. We didn't discuss the case at all.

Bobbye & June Broadway

176

Darling, please tell the fellows that I am highly flattered to be crowned "Queen of Cell 2." However, I'm afraid I didn't have much competition.

Please ask the Fields fellow if he wants any more clothes this week. We can see that he gets them Sunday.

I meant to ask you if the twins are Carl's first children. Are he and his wife on good terms? You know we have some baby things we have never used and we could send something to Carl's wife if you'd like.

That was quite a character that was standing by us Sunday. It's a shame when you have to live so close together that someone has to be like that.

There doesn't seem to be much to write about tonight. I am looking forward to Thursday and I think I will just about die if they call it off.

I'm so proud of you and how wonderful you are being. Darling, things are going to be better than ever when we start our life again.

Love always,
Joyce

P.S. Did you get the Bible?

Wednesday
December 21, 1955

Hi Sweetheart,

These days get longer and longer, don't they? I sure hope tomorrow is the day.

Guess what? You have probably heard by now that "Mac" came up to see me today. I was surprised. He said something about that he was going to try to help me get out for Christmas. I was really surprised. I don't know whether he can help or not. I just hope he won't hinder. He had just come from downstairs and may have heard something and was trying to make like he was going to have something to do with it. You never know. Knowing him like I do, I don't pay too much attention.

I was a little disappointed when I found out this morning that nothing was certain yet about the day. I'm afraid that they don't have court on Friday, so I sure hope it works out for tomorrow.

I understand from what you said this morning that no bond could be set without it going to court. That is a new one to me.

I'm really living on nerves these days, because I keep expecting any minute for something to happen.

Saw the 3 blinks. Hope they mean something but I've about thrown in the sponge. I think somebody is blocking this thing. Somebody that has more power than we have. I don't see how they can keep me up here forever, but I guess if they want to they can.

Darling, keep your chin up for both of us. I love you and wanted to hold you tonight when I saw you down there. I know that you are heartsick as I am.

I'm pretty sure this is the last letter you could get before Christmas. God bless you and oh, how I thank you for being my wife. I know God will have mercy on us and that he is saving that mercy until he sees fit. If it doesn't work out, try to get Pruitt

to get you in to see me other than through the glass. Maybe the preacher could help.

Guess I'll close. Remember, I love you.

Bob

Wednesday
December 21, 1955

My darling,

I know you must really be down in the dumps tonight and I can understand
because I'm at a mighty low ebb myself. Honey, I just can't understand why this
thing has to drag on. Surely you have been punished enough. I have been on pins
and needles all day – thinking that every phone call would be from Pruitt. Finally,
I called Mrs. Fay and then some time later, she called back and said there would
be nothing tomorrow. She didn't know the details. I told her I just had to see you
tomorrow to discuss some business about the house. So she said to come in to
see Mr. Pruitt and he would do what he could.

They are going tomorrow to talk with the judge about bond so that you can spend
Christmas with us. Darling, I just don't think I'm big enough to go it without you.
But honey, I know I must for Ron's sake.

Mimi kept Ron all day today and he had a wonderful time. He was tired and went to
sleep early tonight.

I came home so blue this afternoon that I just sat. I read your letter, cried and sat.
If I could just talk with you some time everything would be wonderful!! Honey,
things don't seem near as bad when we are together.

Earl, Robert and Charles *(Culbreth)* left tonight for Alabama. All the children will
be there to spend Christmas with their mother. The doctor just gives her about six
weeks to live. They are all pretty upset.

Kat and Bud came by and gave me a check for $10.00 on the trailer. You know,
they have already paid $10.00. They are very concerned about you and will do
anything they can.

Darling, Bill Keltner, the music director at church, opened a Christmas card today
and found enclosed a $100 bill. I said I could sure use one like that.

I got Ron's record player from Barbara today. It is very nice. It is in a little grey case that looks like a suitcase. Eight records came with it. They are mostly nursery rhymes – a toy march, etc. I know he will be tickled.

Honey, you asked about Christmas cards. I am sending some but just to people who have been extra nice to us and a few out of town. Most people know the situation and don't expect them.

I looked for a Christmas tree tonight but was too upset. I'll definitely get one tomorrow and I guess Ron and I'll decorate tomorrow night. I hate to see what it will look like.

Sweetheart, I wish I could think of something real encouraging. All I know is that I love you and am praying that you will be home for Christmas.

All our love,
Joyce & Ron

Thursday
December 22, 1955

Hello Sweetheart,

Guess you won't get this letter until Tuesday. By that time either we will have had a wonderful Christmas together or else, well, I'm sure survived.

I'm not going to get my hopes up for Friday because I'm convinced that someone is fouling the deal up in not getting it on the court calendar. I'm surprised that Pruitt hasn't found out who it is yet.

About the house, I don't think we have to take the offer you had. I think that we are just getting to the good time of the year to sell and I think if we sell through the real estate people, we can't take less than $18,500 and without them, $17,500. I'm not too sure about whether we should let it go less than $18,500 for anyone. I think to hold on a little longer.

It's too bad that Buddy couldn't be persuaded to drop the last charge as it, I believe, would relieve the situation. I know though that that would never happen. I guess you think my letters ramble around a lot but I don't think very good these days and have to put down whatever I think when it comes to mind.

You wrote about Ron being so crazy about Bud. I'm glad and yet sorta sad because I'm afraid if this goes on much longer or if I got sent away, that my little boy would soon forget his daddy.

Honey, I asked Carl about the baby things. I told him you would be glad to send a couple of things that you already have. I told him you would send them and just put a card in and sign his name. The address is Mrs. Carl Gaave 928 Van Nuys Ave. San Diego, Calif. Don't give too much away. Someday we may want to start over if I miss too much of Ron's life.

If you should get this Saturday and I'm not there, I know that will be a hard time. Honey, if you don't feel up to it, don't try to come down Saturday night or Sunday. You know I want you but I'm just thinking it might be easier on you if you

concentrated on something else.

Brownie seems to be having a time selling his boat. Hope he can soon get it off his hands.

By the way, the twins are Carl's 6th and 7th. He and his wife are not on the very best of terms. Just so-so.

I'm writing this now after seeing you this afternoon. Honey, I don't know what to say that could express my feelings. I'm brokenhearted and I know that you are. My darling, forgive me for turning away as you left but I was just too full to go any further. You are wonderful the way you hold up. I'm afraid I'm the weak one. I'm so tired though that I just don't have any control.

Darling, I know that you have about all you can bear but you must for you and Ron's sake carry on. Maybe someday I will be able to carry my end of the load again.

Looks like Buddy and his Daddy are determined to try to do something else. It is bad that there are people of this type in the world.

It's hard for me to understand why the grand jury wouldn't either act or not act so something could be done.

Honey, thinking about whatever cash we get out of the house. I think that if the indications are that I might get out in the foreseeable future, we ought to take as much cash as possible and put it in the bank and use it to keep payments up on everything than try to pay one or two things off. It will last a good while and by then my income should be back up pretty fair. We could probably give Pruitt and Raby $500 and keep the rest for a while.

I know that you will get a kick out of Ron's Christmas. See if someone will loan you a flash camera and try to get a picture of Ron and the tree.

Darling, you looked mighty pretty today. I wish that I could have hugged you.

I don't guess there is any need to worry about the Bordeauxes but you might use your own judgement.

You might add in the telegram to Buddy that I hope he enjoys spending Christmas with his children. It's mighty hard not to be bitter when I think of the hurt it is doing to Ron.

Honey, if you decide that you are not up to it, don't try to bother with a tree. I know that it will be hard to do anything. You might get a tiny one and put a small string of lights on it if you think best.

I think the fellows here hated the news I got today as bad as I did. One of them said he was going to look my "friend" up when he got out. This place is pretty blue now. All of the fellows are feeling the pressure of the season.

Maybe if I get out next week we can have a little Christmas then. It will be Christmas to me and I'm sure to you if I can get out.

Was good to see you and Ron tonight. He looked so cute running around. You shouldn't stand there and hold him so long. I'm afraid he'll break your back.

You know, I haven't worried much before about the other charge. I sure hope the judge will treat it as he did the other. What does Pruitt think?

Well, honey, I guess I'll close this and say Merry Christmas and I mean that. Honey, on Christmas morning, you and Ron say a little prayer for me. Remember my dear, I love you with all that is within me.

Love to you both,
Bob

Thursday
December 22, 1955

My Darling,

It is after midnight and I almost didn't write this letter because I know anything I
had to say wouldn't do you much good. I'm just not thinking very well tonight.

I still can't believe that something couldn't be done so you could be home this
weekend. I would give anything in this world but it seems there is nothing.

Honey, I'm sure I wasn't much help when I saw you today. I couldn't say anything
for fear I would cry and I know that would upset you.

Dearest, I know it sounds foolish to say it, but try not to think about Christmas.

Friday
Honey, Ron and I came home and I intended to get a Christmas tree, but just
couldn't. We went to Mimi's for supper. However, I think we are going to have
to stop. It is nice but sometimes she really doesn't have much to eat – chili or
spaghetti, or something like that and if I just had a sandwich for lunch and I'm
not sure of what Ron has had, I feel we ought to eat better. Incidentally, I take my
lunch to work, so you know I don't get stuffed with the kind of sandwiches I make.

Mimi kept Ron for me for a while and I went to town to get a little something
for the people that I am working with. I took Ron to town so you could see him
and then went back to Mimi's. Besides, I didn't want you to see me go to town,
because I knew it would make you feel bad. I did pretty good on the presents –
$.59 for boxes of note paper.

I also got my watch that was being fixed and it didn't cost but $.80. So you can see
that I didn't spend much money.

On the way over to Mimi's, I picked up a pie at Tyler's Restaurant and we ate it
when I got back from town. It was chocolate ice box and honey, it really make

me blue because I thought of how much I wish you could be there with me. But, sweetheart, it wasn't too good.

Darling, I wish you could see Ron on our way to school in the morning. He is usually in a real good mood and sings all the way down. He took presents this morning for his teachers. I got some Avon hand cream from Mamie.

Addie *(Cutulo)* called tonight and was very upset because we couldn't do anything to get you out. She thinks that I'm not really trying because I couldn't explain everything to her about the Grand Jury, etc. She said that she just knew it could be done.

Sweetheart, today is another day and surely there is a possibility of working something out. Honey, I'm just not strong enough to make it through Christmas without you. Honey, it had always meant too much to us and we have had too much fun. I just can't believe that the Lord will want me to do it alone.

The only thing I can think of is the poem that says something about "God has not promised skies always blue... but God has promised strength for the day." Surely, he will give us the strength to see this through. Honey, if I didn't have Him, I would have given up long ago.

We can just thank God that he has given us each other and Ron. That is the most wonderful thing that has ever happened to us and even though we don't have anything else, as long as we can know that we have love, I know we will be strong enough to survive.

Darling, even though Christmas is going to be very difficult, I feel that because we do have our love for each other and for Christ, I know that it will be better than our friends who live in hate. I know God will take care of us.

Sweetheart, I'll be there early Sunday so I can be the first one in.

Yours forever,
Joyce

Friday
December 23, 1955

Hi Sweetheart,

It's about noon and I think I'll start your letter. This is one I hope I don't have to mail. Maybe it is blind faith but I just won't give up hope until 5 o'clock this afternoon. Somehow I just think the Lord will answer my prayers. He said he would in the latter part of Matthew.

I guess this is the hardest time, darling, for all of us. I try not to let it enter my mind but past Christmases keep jumping up and I savor their memory. One of the big disappointments, of course, is to not be able to see Ron on Christmas morning. Of course, my dear, not being able to be with you is the worst of all.

I'm a little surprised that I haven't heard from Daddy this week. Of course, I guess that he figured I'd get out.

If you get this Saturday, you will have a chance to tell me by Sunday what the folks and the Flynns gave us. I know that will be about all but I'll get a kick out of hearing about it. If you think about it, try to bring Ron's birthday pictures with you.

Honey, when you see the match in the window, please know that it is saying Merry Christmas and I love you. Each one I strike I say that. When you throw me a kiss, I know that you are saying the same thing.

I started to write the Judge last night and ask to be released until Monday, just to see if it would do any good. But decided that it might hurt more than help. I wouldn't want anything to upset him.

4:30
I was just sitting here looking at TV and saw Bob Crosby's program. He had all the kids of the staff of his program. Made me feel like I'm sure neglecting Ron. Did you ever take Ron to see Santa? What did he say? Was he afraid?

You know there is a ray of light, maybe this time next week, we will be together.

187

We can hope, can't we?

I guess we are getting stir crazy up here. We are getting so bored that we started playing games. Six of us started playing the old Numbers game and it passed the time for a while and we had a few laughs.

6:30
Well, I've about decided that the judge isn't going to let me out today. I'm just going to get busy and try to get another week to pass. They go pretty slow but I'll make it.

7:30
Guess I better finish this. You looked a little tired tonight. Honey, buck up and be happy. We'll get over this and things will get better and better. I'll bet Ron is excited about Christmas. He looked so cute way down there tonight. I know he must be a bird. I bet he will play that record player until it wears out.

Good night & God bless you both.

Love,
Bob

Friday
December 23, 1955

My Darling,

Somehow or other we are going to live through the next few days and next
year remember it as a horrible nightmare. But, honey, I don't know just how we
are going to do it, except for the Good Lord. Yesterday when I talked with Mr.
Pruitt and with you, I thought it was about the end of the world, and I am sure
you thought the same. But honey, I love you and I love Ron and I know that we
will have a Christmas. Maybe this is done because we have placed too much
importance on physical things and not enough on the real reason for Christmas.

Darling, I thought that you would be interested to know that we have received
98 cards. So you can see that we still have friends. I sent cards to the Counts,
Morrisons *(Sister & brother-in-law)*, Daniel, Deters and Bordens and said, "This is
the time of year for peace on earth, good will toward men. Hope you have a very
Merry Christmas." And, I signed it from all three of us. Of course, I don't think they
have a conscience, so I doubt if it will bother them.

Honey, things were sorta slow at work today. I guess it was because I was so upset
I couldn't do much work. I called the preacher and he called Brautigam and Pruitt
and said they were to do anything they could to get you out. But it is all tied up with
the Grand Jury and there isn't a thing they can do. There was an article in the papers
stating that you could not spend Christmas because the irate father requested a
Grand Jury investigation. I hope it makes Buddy very proud and happy.

And I have had several phone calls asking what they could get for you for
Christmas and I just didn't know what to say. We will have Christmas later, and
really do it up right.

Estelle called me tonight and said that Dave Doggart *(Sister June's ex-husband)*
called and wanted to know how to get in touch with me. He had seen the articles
in the paper and was very concerned and wanted to know if he could do anything.
Estelle said that she didn't tell him anything because she didn't know what our

attitude was toward him. But I told her that Dave knows everybody and his brother and just might know someone who could do some good. I wouldn't object to talking to him at all. Of course, I would just as soon that June didn't know about it.

Well, darling, we finally got our tree up. You would probably be ashamed of it, but Ron and I aren't professional like you are. Honey, they had a tree at Church that they used for a play and weren't going to use it anymore, so I brought it home. It is about six feet tall – sorta flat on one side and not nearly as pretty as the ones you have always gotten, but it was free and something that I could handle myself. It looks alright with the decorations on it. When I picked up Ron from school, I had it in the trunk of the car and he was so excited that he could hardly wait to get home. He laid everything out all over the living room floor and really kept me busy. He just couldn't get things put on fast enough.

Sweetheart, I have to go to town in the morning to get a couple more things. I had bought a pair of bedroom slippers for Mimi and went over there the other night and she had on a brand new pair of bedroom slippers that she had bought for herself. So I guess I will take them back and I haven't bought anything for Brownie yet.

Keep your chin up, honey. It won't always be this way. I love you, my dearest.

Love forever,
Joyce & Ron

Saturday
December 24, 1955

Hi Sweetheart,

It's about 11:30 in the morning and I thought I'd start your letter. I sorta feel like I'm talking to you when I'm writing. It makes me feel close to you.

Honey, today is starting out mighty hard. It is so beautiful outside and I can just picture me with my list running around doing last minute things. Darling, I always enjoyed our wanderings in the car and oh, how I long to be with you today flitting hither and yon.

I have requested a chance to use the phone today but don't have much hope. I'd love to talk with you today. I think if I can make it through today and tomorrow morning and then can see you at noon, I'll survive the rest of it.

Honey, I do wish that the preacher could have come to see me or maybe come the first of next week. I need a little buck up from him.

I guess you will get this Monday and then honey, it will be only three more days if somebody doesn't foul up the works again.

I only hope that if I do get out it, won't be many days before the house can be sold and we can be together.

3:00 PM
I just had an unusual surprise. Dave, our ex brother-in-law, came to see me. He was very nice and I guess told me the same thing that he told you. He said that he saw you yesterday. He had a good suggestion that I'll discuss with you tomorrow.

I just got your letter that you wrote Wednesday. It was mighty sweet. Honey, I know that you are having a rough time of it and it just tears my heart out. It sounds like Ron's record player must be cute and I'm sure he will enjoy it.

Somehow, I think God must be terribly angry with me in not letting me be with you and Ron. It really scares me about the future. For I have prayed nearly every minute for a week for the chance to be home Christmas.

Honey, I will be thinking every minute tonight and tomorrow of you and Ron. And remember every time you see something funny and laugh, you are helping me. Because the hurt I have is not self pity but the agonizing knowledge that I have hurt you and Ron. You will have to be, and you are, mighty big to forgive me for what I have done to you. That is all that I have to live for.

My prayer is that even as a new life was born with Christ on Christmas, a new life will be born for us.

What a thrill I had tonight to see you and Ron. It did me so much good to see you playing with him. My darling, what a special potion God must have moulded into you to make you such a wonderful person. It takes a lot of love, devotion, fortitude and just plain being wonderful to be what you are. Oh, how I love you. I'm picturing in my mind now that you are driving out to the Flynn's and then in a little while, there will be presents for everyone. Have fun, darling. It makes me happy for you to have fun.

Well, I have to close this and soon will be bedded down but not to wait for Santa Claus. But to wait till tomorrow when my wife comes. Good night and God bless you both.

Love,
Bob

P.S. That last match after you put Ron in the car is just a special light of love for you.

Sunday
December 25, 1955

Hi Sweetheart,

Gee, Honey, you coming up here today was about the most wonderful thing that ever happened to me. Before you got here I was sorta down but the minute I saw your sweet, pretty, smiling face, it was Christmas for me. My darling, you are about the most wonderful ray of sunshine that ever came into anyone's life. Every time I see you, I just love you more and more.

Honey, what a surprise. The jacket is beautiful and fits perfectly. I have always wanted one and I'm so proud of it. Tell everyone how much I appreciate it. The yellow shirt is a beauty and I'm glad to get the shorts, handkerchiefs and the foot-warmer shoes. Also the socks. Honey, I'm real tickled with the book. I'm sure I'm going to enjoy reading it. You know this past week I have been reading my Bible a lot and haven't had too much interest in the other kind of books. This one will be just fine.

I gave 4 of the handkerchiefs to the four fellows here with me. They seemed to get a big kick out of them. They sure envy me in having a wife like you and were all as excited about my swell presents as I am.

You sure did surprise me with the jacket. It is beautiful and certainly bought with a lot of faith behind it.

Darling, I'm so sorry Mimi asked you for the money for your gifts. I so wanted to surprise you. I'm sorry it worked out that way because I had such a nice surprise and I wanted you to have a little something that you wouldn't know about. I keep saying that it will be different next year.

I got such a thrill out of hearing about Ron's Christmas. I have told the fellows here about it in great detail. If you think of anything you didn't tell me about, write me, as I can savor each detail.

By the way, you know you told me so many things that I didn't absorb all of it. What did you say my folks sent us?

We had a pretty nice dinner here today. We didn't have pressed pork though it was just a slice of ham. But we had dressing, potatoes, beans, pie, celery, cranberry sauce, pickles and a little candy and a package of cigarettes. It was very nice. Nothing like my sweet wife cooks though.

Say, I forgot to ask you where you and Ron were eating dinner. I hope you didn't wind up in a place like you and I went to on our first Christmas. Remember? You got a bad break with your husband from the first, didn't you?

I'll bet you get Ron in bed early tonight. I know that he will be tired. I expect from the way your eyes looked today that you could stand a little sleep, too. Sweetheart, I want you to eat better and get some sleep. Nothing must happen to the most precious possession I have on earth.

I sure got a kick out of you telling about wrapping presents until 4:45 AM. It sounds so much like you. Another one of the things I love you for.

You better stay away from Jack's. I'm afraid he'll get you off the wagon. Ha! Thank God that's one thing neither of us has to worry about.

As I said today, it might be a help if Buddy would drop the last charge. However, I do believe that it would be wise to speak to Pruitt before making any moves. And besides, I don't want you to put yourself in a position of begging them for anything. Use your own judgement. I don't know either about whether to take advantage of Dave's offer. It would be dirty politics and yet, I've sure been on the receiving end of some mighty dirty stuff myself. Again, use your own judgment and Pruitt's.

Love to you both,
Bob

P.S. The boys said tell you thanks for the Christmas presents. I just happened to think, don't forget to ask Pruitt about whether we need witnesses or not. If so, have him come up Tuesday and I'll give him a list. I sure hope you don't have to work tomorrow. I feel so bad for you to be working and me sitting down. You are mighty brave.

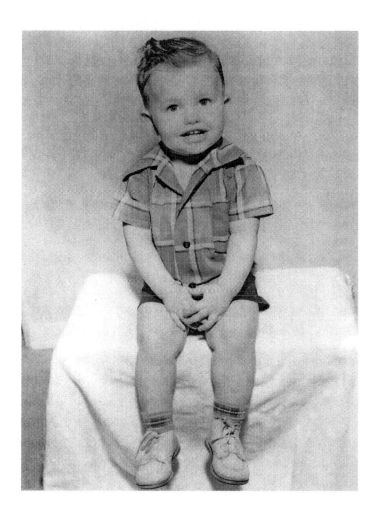

Sunday
December 25, 1955

My dearest,

Well, we've about got this day licked. It hasn't been a very happy one and I'm sure it has been even worse for you. Darling, I know how long the days are for me - so they must be terrible for you.

Honey, I guess by now you have the things we sent you. If the jacket is too big, I can take it back. Darling, I'm sure I told you, but Brownie, the Flynns, Mother and Daddy gave you the jacket. Mamie T. gave you the white handkerchiefs and the McCalls, the socks.

Thank you so much for the pajamas. I really can use them. It gets sorta cold sometimes. And the hose, you know I am always needing.

Dearest, when I left you today, I felt like it was about the end of the world. It was such a let-down feeling – but I guess you know what I mean.

I went to get Ron at the Flynn's – thinking he would probably be asleep – but he wasn't. They gave us a hot dog and we came on home.

Ron has been so excited all day that he has just been running around. But he has been mighty good to be as tired as I know he must be.

I brought Ron home and thought we would take a nap. I got him in bed and just lay down when the Norrises came by. They brought Ron a Davy Crockett holster, coloring book, powder horn and some little cars. He was real tickled with it and I thought it was mighty nice of them. She offered to take care of Ron anytime she could. He wanted to send you a carton of cigarettes but I told him that was impossible. They were very nice and certainly good friends.

While the Norrises were still here, Dave came by. He brought his wife and baby. The wife seems very nice and the little girl is real cute. She looks a lot like Dave – has curly hair and pretty blue eyes. Ron had a time showing her his toys. He didn't

know what her name was, so he said when she picked up a Christmas card off the table, "Somebody bothered your cards."

Honey, after they left, we dressed and were going to eat. I decided we were going to have some sort of Christmas dinner. Well, we rode over to 8th Street to the cafeteria and it was closed. Rode downtown and it was closed. Rode way out the Boulevard and the only restaurants that weren't closed had waiting lines. So it was time to come down and see you. After we left, we finally went to Harry's and had a nice dinner. Honey, it reminded me of the Christmas that we rode all over town looking for a place to eat.

Then darling, we went by Mother's. She was feeling better and we stayed for a little while. Ron was wound up and really showing off.

I wish you could hear Ron sing: "You better watch out – you better don't cry – I'm telling you why – Santa Claus is coming to town." He sang it once and the folks clapped for him so he sang it several more times.

Then honey, we came home. Put on his pajamas and he watched TV for about 30 minutes then went to bed.

I think about you with nothing to do but watch TV and I can't ever seem to find time to watch it. When I am home, I'm so busy I can't see it. But, one of these nights we'll all three just be sitting around watching.

Mother said tonight that when June went out to Betty's – that Betty was crying and Buddy was sick in bed. So their Christmas wasn't too good. I don't know what was wrong with Buddy but I believe your sins will find you out and maybe they are suffering a little for what they have caused us to suffer. You know darling, in last night's paper there was an article stating that judges have freed 200 prisoners for the holidays and to think that someone could be mean enough to keep you up there.

Honey, this is one Christmas we'll have to wipe off our bank of memories and just look forward to next year.

I forgot to tell you today that the Childers sent you some shaving lotion and Bobbye *(Youngest sister)* sent you a blue tie. But I didn't bring them up to you.

I feel that we have been cheated so much. This is the first year that Ron has really understood what Christmas was and really known about Santa Claus and looked forward to it. And, we couldn't enjoy it together. It just doesn't seem fair. Honey, you can't imagine how heavy my heart has been and how weak I felt just knowing that the full responsibility of showing him a good time rested on me.

Darling, sometimes I feel so tired and think how wonderful it would be to just get in the car and ride and have you do the driving. I get so lonesome for your arms around me. I need your love. To think that I ever said, "I can't get any housework done because my husband is home all the time." Boy – just for a chance to have you home again.

I thought I just couldn't make it through today – but I have. So I know the Lord will give us the strength for each day as it comes. And some day darling, we are going to have an opportunity to work and pay Him back for what he has done for us.

Honey, I know you probably couldn't see Ron very good Saturday night but he had two earrings on each ear. One on the top and one on the bottom. He was really a bird.

Ron and I both miss you so very, very much. It is so hard to push myself to do anything without you. I'd like to just crawl in bed and stay there and wake up when this thing is all over.

I love you with all my heart. You are mighty wonderful. I don't know how you have taken what you have but one of these days soon we will be together and everything will be just wonderful. We will realize how beautiful life really is.

Honey, I must be getting tired because I can't even write straight.

So will close with all my love,
Joyce

Christmas, 1955

Monday
December 26, 1955

Hello Sweetheart,

Gee, this has been a long day and it is still just 3:45. It has looked so dreary
outside and there isn't much traffic on the street. In addition to that, I feel like it is
just a lost day because nothing is being done.

You know, you said yesterday that June told you that Betty was upset about the
last turn of events. I wonder how much there is to that. Of course, it could be so
but I just wonder if they didn't know what the old man was doing.

Honey, I have had my jacket and other presents out about 10 times today and
thought how nice they are. In my mind, I sorta open them up like I would presents
under a tree. It makes me feel closer to you.

I still haven't had any mail. The last letter I had from you was written last
Wednesday. I hope it gets straightened out by tomorrow. It really helps to hear
from you.

I'll bet old Ron is giving that record player a fit about now.

I have been thinking about when we get up in the country. I'm sorta looking
forward to it. I want to take you out and teach you to hunt and do some of the
things that can be done up there that we don't have here. I'm going to try to keep
you so busy and happy that you won't miss Miami too much. I just know we
can be happy, darling. Of course, I'll have an advantage over you because I'll be
deliriously happy just to be with you.

Honey, I want you to know that I am well aware of the efforts that you have put out
to try to keep things going so that I might get out. Honey, I'm so thankful because
if it were not for you pushing, I'm afraid I'd be buried up here and forgotten. Just
another thing that I'll have to make up for.

Say, that boy has found him a special place to do his business, hasn't he? I notice that every night he has to go. I get a big kick out of you all in the doorway. I know you must be embarrassed when people pass.

He really scares me, running up the street and around the corner. You'll have to paddle his fanny.

You know, when I look down, I feel like I'm seeing my two diamonds down there on the street. My heart just jumps down there with you. I sure do love you, baby. I hate to think about you having to go to work in the morning. My prayers always include asking God to make it easy on you.

Guess I'll close and say good-night. I love you again and again.

Kiss Ron for me.

Love,
Bob

P.S. Say, would you get the letters quicker if I sent them to the church? Or would you like that? I don't know the address. Whatever you would like best.

Monday
December 26, 1955

My dearest,

When this is all over and we are together again, we are going to have to get our hours adjusted. You're used to going to bed at 9 and I can't seem to get in bed before 12. I was determined I was going to bed early tonight but it is now 11:15.

Well darling, we have had quite a busy day working. I got up at seven this morning so I could get busy. I had so much I wanted to do since I go back to work tomorrow. I washed three loads of clothes, cleaned the house all day long and ironed tonight. The house was really filthy. I don't think I have cleaned the blinds since this whole investigation started. But I feel better knowing things are sorta straight.

Ron has been a living doll today. We have had a big time. He slept until around nine and then we had breakfast. I started to pick up his glass of milk and dropped it. He put his hands on his hips – cocked his head to one side and said, "If you do that again, I'll have to whip you."

Then honey, he wanted to go next door for a while so I went over and asked if he could. But he just stayed about 30 minutes and came home. The kids next door got boots for Christmas and I thought maybe that would get Ron interested in his but he still won't wear them.

Ron and I made some changes today. We moved a bed from the back bedroom into his room. All night long I hear him thump around in that little bed and I just decided to put him in a big bed. Of course, if he wets it the first night, I may have him back in the little one. But I did put a pad on. He is really tickled with it. He wanted to move your bed in there, "because my Daddy never sleeps on it."

The other day, I bought a couple of pillow cases because we were down to just one. These have little flowers on them. Well, I put one on my bed but put a plain one on Ron's bed. Well, he just had a fit. He said, "My Daddy'll tell you – better give me one of those pretty flowers."

Well, anyway, we ate lunch watching the TV and Ron went to bed. Mimi called and wanted us to come eat dinner about three but I told her I couldn't because I had too much to do and besides we wouldn't be hungry that early. So she said to come by for dessert on our way down to see you. Well, she had gotten what they call "snowballs." It is vanilla ice cream covered with coconut with a poinsettia on top and a place for a candle. We lighted them all and Ron sang "Happy Christmas" and blew them out.

Darling, one night I let Ron tee-tee on the street when we went down to see you and now every night he thinks he has to.

Ron and I really have gotten along beautifully today. He has been mighty cute. He has played with his toys and helped me. When I am working he always wants to know "what my can do?"

Honey, Mrs. Berdeaux called and said she had tried to get us to come have Christmas dinner with them. I'm glad she didn't though, because she had the whole family and I wasn't much in the mood. She wants to keep Ron some day this week and I may let her because it will be nice for him.

I sure did miss the mail today. I'm anxious to get a letter from you. I miss hearing from you. Just wish you could get my letters every day. It would be something anyway.

You may want to find a younger wife when you get out. I washed my hair tonight and was looking at all the grey hair!! Wow!! People will be asking if I'm your Mother.

Darling, I can hardly wait until tomorrow when I can talk with Pruitt and see what we can find out. I sure intend that they push this thing. I would like to have a few more details!!

Did I tell you that we had a nice card from the Padgetts saying they were thinking of us and praying for us?

Darling, each day seems like forever but I just know things are going to be better soon. Surely this can't last much longer.

Please take care of yourself. Try to think and plan for what we are going to do when this is all over and try not to worry too much. Everything is going to be all right.

All our love, forever,
Joyce

Tuesday
December 27, 1955

Hello Sweetheart,

Boy, what a thrill to see you today. It just sets my heart singing to see you. Honey, I'm afraid that if you keep getting prettier that the movies will get you.

I got your Thursday & Friday letters today. So you see, I've had an exciting day.

You know I was just thinking if everything goes OK, maybe I can be there when this letter comes. That sure would be a thrill.

I was glad to hear the information about Buddy & Betty. I hope it is the beginning of a change of attitude. This might be wishful thinking but I do wish it would happen. In spite of everything, because Betty being your sister, maybe someday we can be friends again.

I know that Ron is a big shot with his big bed. Our little man is growing up, isn't he?

I know that you appreciate Addie *(Cutulo)* helping us out today as much as I do. She looked to me like that she is under a pretty big strain too. I sure hope everything works out for them.

Saw you tonight and counted 3 blinks. I sure hope that that is the real dope and that they aren't fooling us like they have before. Anyway, here's hoping.

You know, I sure enjoyed the book by Peale that you brought me. It had a lot of good thoughts in it. You will enjoy reading it.

Say, if something should go wrong, see if Pruitt will bring you up again Thursday or Friday. Of course, nothing will go wrong this time, I'm sure.

Don't know anything much so I'll close just saying, I love you and I'm counting the minutes until I can see you and kiss you without an audience.

Love to you both,
Bob

Joyce & Betty Broadway

Tuesday
December 27, 1955

Hi Darling,

How wonderful it was to see you today. Baby, you looked so tired. I'm so
anxious for you to get out so you can get back to being your old self. Honey,
I want you where I can take care of you. I'll admit, it's mighty poor care but I'll
try to do better.

I didn't get a chance to talk with Pruitt again this afternoon. He was gone when I
got back to the office. His secretary said that something definitely would happen
on Thursday. I sure hope she knows what she is talking about. They claim the
whole thing will finish up then.

Mimi offered to pick Ron up from school so I let her and I dashed home to find
three wonderful letters. They were nice long ones and so sweet.

Then I went back over to Mimi's and we had dinner. Elaine *(Brownie's girlfriend)*
was there and all the rest of the family. It was supposed to be a birthday party for
Barbara and she had to work until 9:00 PM. It was very nice. After I went down to
see you, I went back and did the dishes.

Honey, Little Harry was going to a dance tonight but he wasn't going to take Pat.
She was over there to help him get ready and then he took her home and went and
got his girl. We had quite a time getting Little Harry ready. Mimi had made him
a bright red cummerbund and tie. Big Harry insisted that it didn't look like Little
Harry. So Mimi was getting real excited. Anyway, he looked real nice in a new
white dinner jacket.

When we came down to see you, Ron kept hollering, "It's raining, Daddy, and I
don't have no umbrella." He wanted me to stop at the store and buy one.

I hope you saw the lights blink. Maybe it will help you get some rest.

Darling, your folks sent me a nice purse. It is good leather and they sent Ron a

wagon of blocks. I have left all of his Christmas out so that you can see it. It is a little messed up but some of the stuff he hasn't even touched.

I know Dave's suggestion sounds like a good idea but I would like for us to lick this thing fair and clean. We have been hurt mighty bad but that doesn't give us the right to hurt someone else. I think we will be happier and better able to live with ourselves. You probably feel this is easy for me to say since I am out here but I believe if you stop and think, you will feel the same way.

Honey, you know, I still can't believe this has happened to us. It is like a nightmare. I would give anything if we could sell this house and clear enough money so we could get ourselves straightened out. I have an idea that Pruitt is expecting to take every dime we get. He keeps asking me about the house. Of course, I intend that we should pay him whatever he says but it is going to be mighty difficult because we are already up to our ears.

Ron is in bed and I still have to iron a couple of things so I better get started.

It was so good to hold you just for a minute. I love you so very much. Life is so empty without you. Honey, you are everything to me. I hope when you are with me again you won't have such a rude awakening about what a stinker I am.

Yours always,
Joyce

Wednesday
December 28, 1955

Hello Sweetheart,

Well, as I said yesterday, I'm expecting to be home to see the mailman bring this. Boy, has this been a long day. I'm so excited I hardly know what to do. Darling, I just pray that tomorrow will be the day that will bring us together. I wish I could have talked to you today on the phone. I sorta expected someone from the lawyers' office up today but so far at 4 PM, I haven't seen them.

I got your letter today that you wrote Sunday night. It really makes me sad to know I missed Christmas. I'm sure that the good Lord will let us make it up.

I'm so anxious to be with you and Ron that I'm almost jumping from one foot to another.

I'm looking forward to your lights tonight to say that they haven't changed their minds again.

I got a haircut today so I could look pretty in court.

7:15
My darling, if what I think is true, it looks like from no blinks that it is all off again. Honey, if it is, I don't think I can take it. If you will, please have Pruitt, himself, bring you up here. I must talk to him or I just don't know.

A man can only take so much of this and I need to get some information from Pruitt.

Honey, I don't want to sound so down and out but I'm about the end of my rope. I know, dear, that you have had about all you can take, too.

I love you, dear, and I'm praying to God to give you all the strength you need.

Love,
Bob

Wednesday
December 28, 1955

Hi Darling,

It is hard to believe that this is only Wednesday. It seems like it must be Saturday and time to see you again. These Sundays sure do creep around.

Darling, I am quite down in the mouth tonight. I just knew that tomorrow would see us together again. I am really sick because nothing will happen. I know this is really a test of our faith. How thankful I am that you have a strong faith that will see you through. You know there are a lot of people who claim Christ but don't really know Him. I believe you and I are getting to know Him better each day. The Lord uses a lot of people that have been knocked down and I believe when he finally picks us up, he will be able to use us.

Honey, did you know that on the front of the courthouse are lights in the form of a cross? It seems very significant. Christ suffered on the cross for a purpose and surely you are suffering for a purpose.

I know this probably isn't much encouragement to you but you know, if you spend these weeks where you are and everything works out, it is a much shorter sentence than it could have been. And you could have been some place where I couldn't get to see you. So dearest, regardless of how bad things look - it could be worse.

Honey, this guy Pruitt is quite a character. I haven't been able to talk with him today. I called twice and finally Mrs. Fay told me that the Grand Jury would not release your file until Tuesday when they are in session again. So we have another day to look forward to. Honestly, it seems like we live from Tuesday to Thursday to Sunday.

We had dinner at Mimi's. It was a birthday dinner for Barbara. Ron had quite a time helping to blow out the candles. We didn't give presents – just cards – Ron wanted to take his card back.

Honey, Brownie really fixed himself up on this boat deal. He sold his motor and trailer to one man and was supposed to sell the boat to someone else. But the guy

who was to buy the boat never showed up again so he is stuck with just the boat. He really has had a time.

After we left the Flynn's, we rode by the Stone's to see all their Christmas presents. Bud bought Kat a place setting of silver and a pair of those black shorty pajamas, something like my blue ones. Ron and Susan had a big time playing but it made us late coming home. I know I should come straight home with Ron and get him in bed.

Darling, I am so glad you like the jacket. I hope you will tell me if you don't or if it doesn't fit so we can exchange it.

I have been wanting to save my pajamas to wear when you can see them but if it turns cold, I may be forced to wear them.

Did I tell you I got the refund on the house insurance? It was $84 something. I deposited it with my paycheck today. Since the bank is so far away from work, I have been "banking by mail." I had them send me some deposit slips and today, I had to call and ask them to send me a couple of checkbooks. Oh yes, I sent the house payment off today and the first of next week I'll have to pay the air conditioner, piano and I'm not sure what else. This will be the last payment on the piano.

Honey, you said something about Ron running up to the corner. He goes up to look at the Christmas tree and he is playing a game. I am supposed to run after him. He gets quite a kick out of being chased, you know.

I thought once about having you send the letters to the church because I would get them at noon. The only trouble would be on Saturday. I wouldn't get any mail. The address is 151 NW 60th Street. The letter you write on Thursday and mail Friday, though, send to the house so I will get it on Saturday.

I understand Guy's case is coming up Tuesday. Can't figure out why there was no follow up on the examination for him. They haven't said.

I hope you got the information today about your case. I was really upset because I had blinked the lights last night but Pruitt seemed confident that you were going to court tomorrow.

Darling, my prayers are with you constantly that the Lord will take care of you and bless you and strengthen you.

All my love, forever,
Joyce

Bud and Kat Stone

Thursday
December 29, 1955

Hello Sweetheart,

3 o'clock
This has been a pretty bad day. I wonder what happened? Of course, I haven't
heard a word so I just don't have any idea of what the situation is. You know it is
hard to understand just what the Lord has in mind for me. This, "you are going to
get out today – no, it's next week" stuff – is just about to wreck me and I'm sure
that it's about to do the same to you. One of the worst things about this place is
the lack of communication. I did get 2 letters today – the ones you wrote Monday
and Tuesday.

You know honey, I've never been a prude but you just can't imagine the foul
language and talk that goes on here. It almost makes me sick to have to listen to it.

Gosh baby, you must get tired listening to me complain and I get tired of writing
like that. I never hear any good news. It's always, well, another deal fell through.

I wish the preacher or Bill *(Culbreth)* would come to see me. I need a little spiritual
uplift. I spend lots of time reading my Bible but I make a poor preacher for myself.

For your own peace of mind, you ought to stop calling Pruitt and just forget about
this mess and go about your life and when and if I get out of here, I'll call you. I
know you will say, "I can't do that," but you have got to go on and Ron needs you
so much.

Honey, of course I don't have any idea what has happened, but if they are trying
to get something else going and it concerns the 24th Avenue folks *(Berdeaux)*, be
sure to see them and do everything possible to make sure they won't do anything.

If you would get in touch with Richard Crowe and make a picture of the Christmas
tree and of you and Ron and could work it out in the dark room. I know that he would
be glad to. Maybe Betty Ellis could, through Bobbie, put you in touch with them.

If it looks to you like I'm here for a while, and I don't know how it could look otherwise, please try to have a little picture taken of you and Ron and send it to me. My darling, it would mean so much to me because I could look at it and talk to you a little bit.

Guess this is the last letter you will get before New Year's Eve. I can only say that I hope 1956 will be better to us than 1955. I wish that if you are awake at 12 o'clock Saturday night, you would get a picture of me out of the dark room and give it a kiss and I'll be awake kissing you in my mind and thinking and loving you with all that is within me.

Ron looked cute running around tonight. You will have to stop wearing such tight skirts as it looks like he can about outrun you. Guess he'll outrun me by the time I see him again.

Darling, the *(Orange Bowl)* parade will be going Saturday night and I'm afraid you would have trouble getting down at 7:00. If you want to look at 4:30 and then you won't have to come back. I worry about you driving with all the drunks on the street. I'll look at both times. If you have trouble seeing a match at 4:30, don't worry because I'll be looking. If things look fairly encouraging, bring an extra sweater or coat and just drape it over your right arm.

Kiss Ron for me.

Love,
Bob

Happy New Year

Thursday
December 29, 1955

My dearest Bob,

This is the day that I thought would really be a red letter day in our lives. But I guess I'll learn one of these days to quit having too much hope. Darling, I kept thinking all day, how wonderful it would be to hold you once again. I miss your love so very much.

I didn't hear anything from Pruitt today and I didn't call him. I thought I would give him a day off and tomorrow I will call and ask him all the questions that I need to and see what information I can get to bring to you on Sunday. I know you hate the thought of one day going by and us not pushing it. But I am sure he is working on it and I hate to aggravate him too much. He promised he would push for something before the weekend. I hope he knows what he is doing.

Dearest, I got the insurance policy from Neil today. It is with Glen Falls Insurance Company and will cost us $97.80. Neil says he thinks this will be permanent but if they should cancel he will just put it with another company and keep us covered until the house is sold. He sent the policy to Independent and sent us a duplicate. He really has been very nice and I do appreciate it.

Jeannette called the other day and said they were so upset when they read the article in the paper last week. They wanted us to know that they are still praying for us.

Honey, Bill Culbreth came back from Alabama today. He said they put his mother in the hospital in Dothan. Of course, there is nothing they can do but just try to keep her alive and comfortable. They are all pretty upset about it.

I think I told you that Earl, Charles and Robert had a wreck and turned the car over on their way up to Alabama. Bill drove Charles' car back and it is really a wreck. They pushed the top out just enough so they could bring it home to be fixed.

You mentioned Ron and the big bed. Do you know he has wet the bed every night since I put him in it? So last night, I made him sleep in the little bed and he wasn't too happy so maybe he'll be alright tonight.

I don't care where we go from here as long as we are together. I'll have to admit that I hate to leave Miami and particularly this climate but we can be happy anywhere. If you have any preference it is alright with me. The only reason I liked the sound of South Carolina was that it closer to Miami and maybe I could come back to visit some. Honey, I wish I could say that I'm glad to leave and it doesn't worry me, but darling, it is home and regardless of the unpleasant things that have happened, we have a lot of pleasant memories too. But home is where you are and we will have a lot of fun making new friends.

Honey, did I tell you that Mimi gave me a new razor called the Circlette? You aren't supposed to be able to cut yourself and so far it has worked.

This big shot son of ours thinks I am supposed to go to bed when he does. I have to be real quiet until he gets to sleep or he will call out "Mommie, what you doing?" The other night he came out in the kitchen after I thought he was in bed and put his hands on his hips and said, "What you doing in this kitchen? You supposed to be in bed." He really is growing up, honey.

Tonight we ate dinner at the store – went down to see you and rode out to Sears to exchange the cowboy suit that Mimi gave him. However, they didn't have on to fit him so they refunded the money. Guess I will have to look around for another one.

Mimi got the pictures back from Ron's birthday party. They are real cute. I'll bring them Sunday.

Honey, I'm afraid we won't get down Saturday because of the parade but I know you will understand. It is just too much to try to bring Ron down by myself in all that traffic.

Love forever,
Joyce & Ron

Friday
December 30, 1955

Hi Sweetheart,

Gee, I sure enjoyed your letter I got today. It was the one you wrote Wednesday and I got a little news from it concerning what had happened that I didn't go to court Thursday. I'm afraid our friend isn't very good for delivering information. I feel a little relieved although I wonder why the delay. I'll just keep hoping.

I'm sure sorry that Brownie got messed up on his boat. He should have held on until he had both men together.

I'm surprised that Guy's deal is going on. However, I understand that the deal goes through and then they have the examination. I sure wish that it had waited until I get through. Of course, at the rate I'm going that could be a long time.

I'm tickled that the mail has gotten a little better here. I'm getting your letters the next day after you mail them this week.

I've had a terrible headache today and it will be tomorrow before I can get any pills. You see, you order one day and you get whatever they decide you should have the next day. By that time, you've got something else. It's really great.

Honey, you'll never know how much your letters mean to me. I really enjoy every morsel of news that you write about and try to picture in my mind just how you and Ron look as you do the things that you write about.

I put out a big wash this morning and it helped pass the time a little bit. I'm getting pretty good. The only thing is that I'm afraid that some of my things have that tattle-tale grey.

Say, did you ever get the brakes fixed, honey? You know, baby, when I look out and see the street are wet or think about the drunks driving, I get sorta scared because nothing must ever happen to you or my boy. You realize that you are my entire life and I couldn't stand for anything to happen to you. Be careful.

Baby, you are a mighty good preacher. The first of your letters I got today meant a lot to me. I have found another wonderful chapter in the Bible for you to read. I think it is talking to us. Read John: 14 – especially verse 14 & 18.

As you say honey, we have our faith and I'm mighty sure mine is much stronger than ever. I know because when the disappointments come, it's rough for a short time and then it eases off as soon as I let God have full sway.

Hug our boy for me,

Love,
Bob

Take special care of yourself today as the traffic will be heavy. Also, I want you to know on New Year's Eve that I love you just a little bit more, if that is possible.

If Ron has his cowboy outfit available, let him wear it in the afternoon if you come at 4:30 sharp instead of 7:00 to avoid the traffic.

Just remember I love you.

Friday 8:45 PM
December 30, 1955

My dearest,

I do believe this is the earliest I have been able to sit down and write to you since
you have been gone. Ron is in bed, but not asleep and I decided I had better be
quiet so he would go to sleep. He thinks I am supposed to go to bed when he
does. He keeps calling out to me, "Do you have your jamas on, Mommie?" "Have
you rolled your hair?"

Honey, there just aren't words to tell you what I am feeling in my heart tonight. I
just wonder how much more we can take. I try to tell myself not to get my hopes
built up but I just can't help it. I know what a let down you must have had because
I can hardly stand it and I can pick up the telephone any time and call to see what
is going on. However, it is difficult to talk with Mr. Pruitt. He usually isn't in and
then has Mrs. Fay call me back. However, since nothing much is happening, I
guess she can tell me as well as he can. Darling, they have been working like mad
on it this week. It is just tied up in the Grand Jury and there is nothing they can do.
It really breaks my heart that there can be so many delays.

When I got your letter today, I was quite upset to find that you hadn't been told
what was going on. I guess I can't count on anyone.

Darling, I hadn't intended to eat at the Flynn's tonight but she insisted. We had a
pretty good supper. I think she brought it from the store – roast beef with noodles
–squash –baked potatoes & beets.

It is about time to take Ron back for his other polio shot and I think I am going
to ask the doctor about some vitamins – calcium or something. He isn't drinking
much milk – maybe a glass a day and I think he needs something. Now don't
worry, honey, he is far from being sick but I just feel that he needs his milk.

Mimi wasn't feeling too good tonight. She has had a cold.

Honey, I understand the parade is to break at Flagler & 8th, so I think I will take

219

Ron down and watch from there. I don't care a thing about going but I believe he will enjoy it.

We had a beautiful card from Lillian Padgett. Thought maybe you would like to read it. It is titled on the front, "Have Faith."

Faith is a wonderful thing.
It can move mountains if it is strong.
It can bring comfort when things go wrong.
Faith is looking beyond today.
It can bring sunshine when skies are gray.
It can bring hope for a brighter day.
Faith is believing whatever comes.
It can give strength for what we must bear.
It can bring peace and dispel despair.
Faith is trusting in One greater than we are.
It can show the way through the darkest night.
May it be your shield and your beacon light.
Keep faith and know that God is with you.

I wish I knew something to say but I believe the words of that card. We must have faith. The Lord is with us and everything will be alright.

Honey, your letters are so sweet. I'm saving them so you better be careful what you say.

I know that you want to see Pruitt and I want him to go to see you but honey, he moves when the spirit moves him. I hope maybe he did go up today.

Tomorrow will be an awfully long day just waiting for Sunday and two hours with you. Those are the two shortest hours of the week.

Yours forever,
Joyce

Card from Lillian Padgett

Saturday
December 31, 1955

Hello Sweetheart,

Well, this isn't exactly the finest way that I know to spend New Year's Eve. But, on the other hand, I guess it could be worse. I'm just having a hard time right now figuring out how.

Glad to see you all down there this afternoon. It's sorta cold so I'm sure that you weren't interested in staying down for the parade. I'd sorta like to be sitting in the living room looking at it on TV. Then we could have a picnic and Ron could help you bring in the tray.

Darling, I'm sure looking forward to tomorrow. You can't imagine how thrilled I am to see you on Sundays and every evening. These are the high points of every day. Everything in my thoughts go around before and after I see my wife. When it gets 7:00, I have to nearly fight my way to the window. There are about 8 or 10 who are there ready to watch. You just didn't know how cute you are, did you?

We nearly froze up here last night. I sure don't like to see cold weather here with this one blanket.

You know, speaking of Ron wetting the bed. Maybe you have a good piece of psychology in having both both beds. If he wets the big one, make him sleep in the little one a night. It might help. Of course, it might come to the point for a while where we will have to get him up about midnight and let him go to the bathroom. You notice I say we because I'm afraid you wouldn't wake up. Ha! Then too, he shouldn't drink so much after supper.

I'll try sending this to the church and see how it works out. If you don't like this deal, you can let me know and I'll change.

I love you dear, and love that little boy too. Good night, my love.

Bob

Saturday
December 31, 1955

My darling,

It is almost midnight and another year is about to begin. My darling, how
lonesome I have been for you!! Today, I have really felt like I was all alone but now
that everything is quiet and I am home, I feel very close to you. And even though
we are apart, I know we are beginning a new year together.

Happy New Year, my dearest... and I know this will be a very happy year for us. It
isn't beginning too well but it won't be long before we are together and everything
is wonderful.

Seems like I have kept busy all day, although I really haven't done much. I washed
this morning and straightened up the house. Then I got Ron all dressed up and
took him down to have his picture made. They wanted $10 for one 8x10, so I
decided that it wouldn't be but a week or so and you could make one or I would
ask Richard Crowe to make one. It is foolish to pay that much and we just can't
afford it.

Honey, we ate lunch at Royal Castle and fooled around town a little. I went by the
station and had the car checked then we went home and got cleaned up to go to
the parade.

The parade broke up right in front of Lynn's, so we got chairs and sat there. I took
a blanket to wrap around us and we had quite a time. Ron was really excited about
everything. One of the floats had a real cow on it and he thoroughly enjoyed it. The
cow mooed just as it got to us and he just squealed. He was very upset because he
couldn't ride on the floats. He wanted me to ask the man if he could ride.

I hated so bad to go to the parade but felt like I ought to for Ron's sake and I am
glad I did. He was so excited he could hardly sit still. He would grab hold of my
face and turn it around so I could see. He asked a lot of questions and if I didn't
answer right away he would say, "Talk to me." He is quite a character, darling. We
have a time together and I am so glad I have him. Honey, I realize how lucky I am.

223

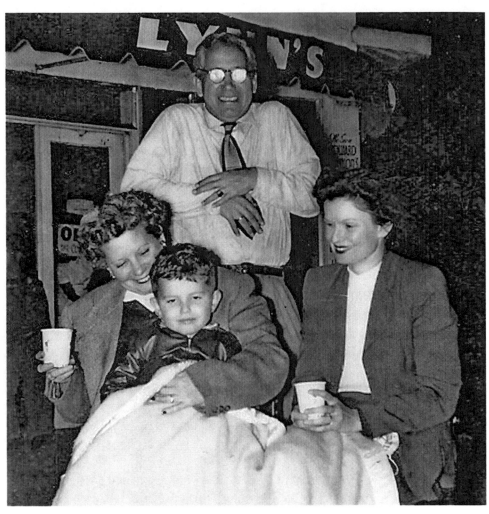

Mimi & D-Dad Flynn with Ron & Joyce
Orange Bowl Parade, Miami, 1955

I feel so guilty because I have everything and you have nothing. But some day I will make it up to you.

That clock is rolling around toward twelve and I wish I had you here in my arms.

This new year is going to find us happier than we have ever been in our lives. We are going to have more love for each other and for other people and certainly we are going to have more love for the Lord.

Those verses you have told me to read mean a great deal to me.

Happy New Year, my dearest. May it be the happiest year we have ever spent.

Yours forever,
Joyce

Sunday
January 1, 1956

Hi Sweetheart,

Baby, I so enjoyed the time we had together this afternoon. It means so much to me to see you and it leaves such a terrible emptiness when you leave. I'm very sure that there are not many loves like ours and I'm so thankful for it.

Well, my prayer shall be that this week will wind the deal up. It will be heaven on earth when I hold you in my arms again.

I went to bed right after you left. I have had a cold for about 3 weeks and I seemed to have a high fever for quite a while this afternoon. However, I covered up and sweated it out and feel better tonight.

I sure appreciated the books and paper, but listen, I think I have enough books for a while. We were just saying this afternoon that we were pretty well supplied and there is no need of you buying anymore for a while. I do want the paper though and I sure enjoy the Coronet and Digest. So you take that other money and buy a little something for you and Ron. When I run out of books, I'll let you know.

Baby, you looked good enough to eat today but please take care of yourself. I don't like to see circles under your eyes. I want to always see a smile on your face and a twinkle in your eye.

I sure wish I knew that I was getting out this week. I would say keep all the insurance with Independent. However, if I get out before too long and can get a job, I can always revive as much as we want to. So you just use your judgement. I know that you will need every penny you can save.

I certainly never thought I'd see a day like this. I have always thought that if I could worry about the money, you would have enough other things to worry about.

7:15

Been feasting my eyes on the most beautiful, wonderful woman in the world and the sweetest little boy that ever had such a sorry husband and Daddy. He looked cute running around like a little ant. I think he has got your number about that doorway down there.

Well, I don't know much so I'll close. I love you so much and can't wait until I get a chance to show you by the kind of living I'll be doing from now on. Be sweet.

Love,
Bob

P.S. Is is time to take Ron back for his polio shot?

Sunday
January 1, 1956

Hi Darling,

It was so good to see you today. You looked so nice in your blue sweater and yellow shirt. We could have gone most any place with you so dressed up.

Honey, there really isn't much to write about after having just seen you but I did think I would get a note started and finish it later.

After leaving you, I went by Mother's and she hadn't put Ron to bed so I brought him on home. She had some fried chicken left from dinner and I ate some of that. I called Mimi and told her I had to bring Ron home to bed and couldn't come over. I was glad because they had a big crowd over and I wasn't much in a party mood.

Honey, I forgot to tell you that Florence *(Mimi's sister)* gave me two bottles of pills. One is calcium and the other is some sort of bone medicine. It is supposed to make me feel real good. You better watch out – I'm going to be so strong you won't be able to handle me!! Ha!!

Honey, you looked so thin today. I wish I could slip in a chocolate ice box pie or chocolate cake. Maybe that would fatten you up a little.

I hear ole "Ronnie" getting up so I guess I'll have to finish this later.

10:35
Here I am back again. Ron is all tucked in. The house is sorta straight and I've dampened some clothes to iron tomorrow. So I can quietly think of my husband and feel very close.

You know, I think of you all day long but I really feel the closest to you early in the morning when things are sorta quiet and late at night after Ron is in bed. When Ron is up, there isn't much time for thinking.

Honey, we ate supper at home tonight. I fixed those chicken pot pies and Ron really seemed to enjoy it.

Then we dressed and came down to see you. In case you were wondering what Ron was doing running around – he was playing that he was a monkey and he was hunting for food. The fireplug was a drinking fountain. He is always playing games like that and wants me to participate.

Don't ever think for a minute that Ron is forgetting you. He talks about you a lot. For instance, on TV this afternoon he saw something he didn't like and he said, "I don't like that. My Daddy doesn't like that either." All day long he is constantly mentioning you. He told someone the other day that his Daddy's name was Bob.

Honey, Ron can always tell when I'm tired and upset and he'll hug me or kiss me and say, "You want my Daddy to come home?"

Whenever we get in the drugstore, Ron always wants a penny to call up his Daddy. He goes in the phone booth and puts the penny in – dials – and then talks to you. He tells you about what he has been doing and tells you to hurry home.

Darling, tonight I went to church. I took Ron to Mimi's and Barbara kept him because Mimi had a cold. I went down to Central. I wanted to hear Dr. Angell. Honey, I heard part of his sermon this morning on the radio on my way down to see you. It was really good. He was talking about a pattern for the new year and the first thing was to hold no hatred in your heart – only love. You know, that is a good one for us. But it is really the thing to do because I know how upset I am inside when I let any hate creep in. So really it does me more harm that it does the people I hate.

Anyway, tonight he preached on some questions to ask ourselves. First of all, "Do we have any habits in our lives that should be given up or changed?" Then, "What is our code of living? Do we love one another – do unto others as we would have them do unto us?" And last, "Is our soul right with the Lord?" Honey, he was as good as I have ever heard him and I really enjoyed it.

I slipped in the back door of the center section and sat in the back. No sooner had I sat down than Miller Walton moved over and sat beside me. He was very nice. Nothing in particular, just friendly. He said when I left, to let him know if he could do anything. I didn't see anyone else to talk to.

Honey, for the last couple of Sundays when I have been up to see you, there has been a nice-looking woman and young girl waiting. Today she saw in my things the "Open Window" and she asked if I went to a Baptist church. Then she said her name was Tucker and she goes to Central. Her son is in 21-S. She didn't tell me why or anything about it. But tonight she sat right in front of me in church and when the invitation was given, she went down to rededicate her life. Honey, my heart really went out to her because I know in her heart she must feel that there has been something wrong with her life and her influence or her son wouldn't be in the trouble he is in. And I feel the same way. But I know the Lord will give us another chance and help us live closer to him. I didn't mean to preach a sermon, but I just got carried away.

Darling, they wouldn't let me leave the pictures for you but said I could mail them so I put them in the letter I had in my pocketbook to mail. You should get them the first of the week.

I checked on your money and you have a little over $15 so you are alright.

I went back over to Mimi's and got Ron. Then we went by the grocery store and I bought a few things for tomorrow and some dog food.

Honey, seeing you really does things to me. Umm... I thought about hanging out the red light but instead put on my red pajamas and went to bed by myself. What a life!!

Incidentally, I'll tell you something that I had meant to tell you today. Remember the Sunday before or after our anniversary when you asked me if things were like they were nine years ago? Well, if I blushed, I had a reason to. It was time and "it" hadn't come. In fact, "it" didn't come at all last month. I was nearly pulling my hair out because I figured with our luck like it has been, I was probably fixed up good. So I called Dr. Holmes and he said that nerves and upset very often cause that. But everything is alright now so I can breathe again. I didn't want you to worry until I was sure there was something to worry about.

I have written quite a book tonight but before I close, honey, I am enclosing a poem that was in the church bulletin. I want to save it and keep reading it to myself all year to remind me of my New Year's resolutions.

Darling, did you know that you are everything to me? Honey, I don't know how you have put up with me but I promise to be a better wife in '56. I love you, my dearest, with all my heart.

I'm yours forever,
Joyce

A New Year's Wish

To be of greater service, Lord,
A closer student of Thy Word;
To help to bear a brother's load;
And cheer him on the heavenly road,
To tell the lost of Jesus' love,
And how to reach the home above;
To trust in God whate'er befall,
Be ready at the Master's call,
For any task that He may give;
And thus thru all the year to live
For Him who gave Himself for me
And taught me that my life should be
A life unselfish, not self-willed,
But with the Holy Spirit filled.

—Selected

Monday
January 2, 1956

Hi Sweetheart,

3:00 PM
I'm sitting here trying to look at the game on television. I can't keep my mind on the game for thinking about you. It is such a beautiful day outside and I know that you and I would be doing something to enjoy it if we were only together. You know, I'll be glad to see the last of the holidays. They are mighty long and rough especially without the girl that I love.

I'd give anything if this was another visitors day. It just does me so much good to see you and talk with you.

I guess all our "good" friends are having a big day today.

Honey, let's double up on our prayers that this week might be the last one like this. I sure hope that someone can move the Grand Jury into releasing this file so that the thing can get underway. It looks like that if they need the file, they could release it for a couple of days and then get it back if needed.

Don't forget to write Cecil concerning the group insurance I have with the company. I hope that he will start the Hudson once in a while so that it will run when I need it.

You know, I'd sure love to be able to spend a week or so at whatever town we are going to before we sell the house. That way we would know whether we could rent a house furnished or not. Seems to me like it is about time our luck changed so something could work out.

7:30
Oh baby, I felt so bad when the car wouldn't start tonight. All I could do was stand there and look. Honey, do you think I'll ever be good for anything to help you again? It makes me hate myself for what I'm doing to you. Try to find a place in your heart to forgive me.

If it is the battery that is bad, try the charger and if that doesn't help, you may have to go to Hi-Volt on 7th Avenue and get a new one. If it was just hard to start, tell Jack to check the points.

I appreciate you coming around again to show me it started. Who was that that pushed you – Brownie?

Darling, I love you and my heart is broken that I have done this to you. Every night I pray to God to give you an extra portion of his love to cloak you to make up for the heartache I have caused you.

Guess I'll close just saying again, I love you, I love you.

Bob

P.S. If you haven't done so lately, call Raby please. I forgot to ask you about her Sunday.

Monday
January 2, 1956

Hi Sweetheart,

Right now I'm watching "I Love Lucy" and wonder if you are. I am really tired tonight and it was good to get Ron in bed and relax for a few minutes while I write to you.

Honey, I know you were worried tonight when I had car trouble and you were standing up there watching and couldn't do a thing to help. The battery was dead. I haven't had any trouble but planned to put the charger on tonight. Guess I should have done it last night.

I walked around to the filling station and there was only one man there and I didn't know him. He said he couldn't do a thing to help me. So I called the Flynns and Little Harry and Pat came in Brownie's car and pushed us off. Now I have the car in the garage with the charger on it so I can get to work in the morning. If it doesn't charge up good, I'll go by Hi-Volt and see if we need a new battery.

This morning Ron got up and we had breakfast. He wanted me to eat some oatmeal and I said I didn't feel like it. So he kisses me and tells me I'd feel better and to eat some oatmeal.

I mowed the lawn today!! All of it!! You know, I told you I had mowed out the front a few weeks ago and really just intended to cut the back but decided while I was at it, I might as well do the whole thing. Whose idea was it to buy a big lot? I really didn't mind though. It did me good to be outside and to get some exercise.

We ate lunch at home in front of the TV. Then we rode downtown to mail your letter. I figured this being a holiday, it would go quicker from the main post office.

We rode by the Flynn's store to get some film and flashbulbs and sat around and talked a while. Someone had taken Harry to the ball game so Mimi was working for him.

Then Ron and I came home. I put him in bed but it was late and he never did go to sleep. I washed the car and cleaned the house and we came down to see you.

Honey, Ron hasn't touched his boots until today and this afternoon he came out with them in his hand and said "I can wear these?" Mimi had just told me today to take them back and exchange them if he wasn't going to wear them. He must have heard her talking.

Bobbie Stewart called and I told her that you had received a card last week. She says she has written you every week. Have you received them?

You know, honey, we may have lost a few friends but we have an awful lot that are standing by us and I sure am thankful for them.

My prayers – my thoughts – my love – are with you always.

Joyce

P.S. Took pictures of the Christmas tree tonight. Sure hope they come out. I'll send them to you if I get them before Sunday.

Tuesday
January 3, 1956

Hello Sweetheart,

Well, it's a little after 4 and I thought I'd start your letter. This has been another long day. I believe that every day gets a little longer. I sorta thought that the preacher would come up today but I guess not.

Gosh, I'd love to be able to see you and talk to you. I'm anxious to know if anything is going on today. I'm looking forward to tonight to see if there are any blinks. Course, I'm trying not to count too big or anything.

Gee, I hope you don't have any more trouble with the car. You better carry a little money with you. I know that you usually don't have much but you may get caught out sometime and need to get a taxi or something.

You know, honey, I have such a hungry, gnawing feeling to see you and to be able to see Ron. You know, it has been seven weeks since I saw him and it just about tears the inside out of me to think about it. I just thank God that I can see you once in a while.

7:30
Well, I guess there's nothing stirring from the absence of blinks. I sorta figured that you might not call Pruitt today, and I'm sure that he wouldn't call you.

You all looked mighty sweet as always. Honey, you should have heard the concern expressed by about half a dozen of the fellows when you were a few minutes late. I told them that I imagined the Orange Bowl traffic held you up.

I was glad to see the car start without any trouble. I sure hope that doesn't happen again.

I wish I could think of something to tell you but I'm sort of a dry well. The routine is right much the same. I've been in here so long that only 3 out of the 32 men who were here when I came in are still here. I'm about to become an old timer.

Next Thursday will make 49 days. That's a long time, huh?

Well, I'll close and say keep smiling, baby, and hug Ron for me. I love you.

Bob

Tuesday
January 3, 1956

Hi Darling,

Thought I would try to type this letter tonight and maybe you could read it a little better. I am really bushed tonight and so I doubt if I will make much sense.

I know that you wondered tonight why I didn't stay long. But, as you could probably tell, Ron was tired and fussy. He didn't want to stay. He wanted me to hold him. And, he kept talking until I was so nervous I could scream. So, I knew that you would understand.

Honey, I am so sorry that I was so late. Lloyd Rodgers came by the house just as I was getting ready to leave. I told him that I was just leaving but he stayed and talked and talked. He was very interested. I guess it was the first time I have talked to him since you have been up there. I understand that they keep sorta close touch with the Stewarts, though. He cannot understand why you cannot be out on bond and it is difficult for me to explain. He said that he'd seen Art Deters and that Art thought you were getting a raw deal. He said Art was very nice and even though he was upset at the first of the thing, he is rather sympathetic toward you now.

It was nice to get your letters at church today. I read them over and over and then had all afternoon to think about them and when I got home, I read them again.

I have been meaning to ask you if you watched the Orange Bowl parade. They were having a show at the stadium tonight and I thought about taking Ron, but finally decided we were too tired to enjoy it.

Honey, I talked with Genevieve this morning and asked about the preacher getting up to see you. But, of course, I don't know. He looked so bad Sunday night. They are really limiting him to the hours he puts in and the things he does. I hope maybe he will get up there this week.

You were talking about my waking up to take Ron to the bathroom at midnight... Just don't kid yourself, honey, I am just getting in bed about that time. I stay up

until I am real sleepy and tired and then I don't get in bed and just lay there and think. It's mighty lonesome without you. I can't help sometimes looking over and just wishing you were lying there beside me.

I won't bring any more books. But, don't worry, I haven't been buying those books. Once in a while I will buy one if I see something that looks good. But, most of them Mimi has given me from the store. People bring books in there and exchange them and so she insists that I take some to you. Also, a few Sundays, she has refused to let me pay for the papers. She says that is the least they can do.

Honey, I know you hate to think of my letting any of the insurance go, but I believe it is the sensible thing to do. Even when you do get out, it is going to take a while for us to get straightened out and we are going to have to cut expenses some. I haven't decided definitely yet and haven't talked with Joe, but I will probably let the policy on you and me go. We will still have plenty of insurance.

I forgot to tell you what happened last night. You know Ron's favorite doorway? Well, they have a little opening for mail and so what does he do but stick his "fawnfee" in there and we could look through the window and see it laying on the floor, but couldn't get it. He nearly had a fit but I found him another one when we got home and I don't think he will be doing that again.

Could you tell the outfit that Ron had on tonight? He had on his pajamas, boots and jacket. He was quite a bird. He seems to like his boots now and I sure am glad.

You asked about Ron's polio shot. Yes, it is time and I will probably take him this weekend.

I am so looking forward to the day when we can be together again. It will almost be like getting married all over again... except that we have a three-year-old child.

You know, sometimes when I come down to see you at night there is a parking place between two cars, but I'm always afraid to try to park. I can feel all those eyes peering down at me and I know I could never get it parked.

Darling, stay sweet for me. Ron says to tell you to hurry home.

I know that it is rough, but the Lord gives me strength to do the things I have to do and dearest, I pray daily that he will give you the strength for what you have to endure. One of these days it will all be over and we can start living again.

Yours forever,
Joyce

Wednesday
January 4, 1956

Hi Darling,

Just a note while I have a minute to explain something to you. State Farm canceled our car insurance and I have been having a little trouble getting some insurance. Allstate, which I believe is the next cheapest will not insure us. Finally, Neil Coates said that he would try to get us insurance but that it would be much easier if the car were in my name since no insurance has been canceled against me.

So I called Pruitt and thought that maybe he would bring me up so I could get you to sign over the title, but he said if I would send the title to him that he would have someone bring it up so you could sign it over. I knew that you would figure I was having it done, but honey, I did want you to know why. I hadn't written you about the insurance because I thought I could get it straightened out and you wouldn't have to worry about it. I had planned to tell you after it was all over.

Don't worry, honey, everything will be alright. Neil said that he would keep the car covered until we could get straightened out.

I am not going to insure the Hudson until it is necessary. I hope that is alright with you. But, you know, it costs money and I really don't have the money to insure both cars now.

Please don't worry about this because it will all be taken care of. Neil has been mighty nice.

I had thought about asking Pruitt about a power of attorney thing so that if anything else developed, I could take care of it. But when I called him today he sorta gave me the brush-off and didn't seem to want to bother with it.

Keep sweet and know that I love you with all my heart.

Joyce

Wednesday
January 4, 1956

Hi Sweetie,

Not much news tonight since I wrote you this afternoon.

This has been a rather uneventful day. Pruitt has no news for us. He just can't
seem to move anything but says he is working on it.

Honey, we haven't been to the Flynn's this week because Mimi has had the flu and
I figured we had better stay away.

Ron seemed to be tired tonight. So after we left town, we came on home and I put
him to bed. He still has a cold, although it is getting better. On the way home he
was having a fit for some ice cream, so we turned on the heater and sat in the car
and ate a hot fudge sundae.

I wrote Cecil today about the insurance so maybe I will know something by
Sunday.

Honey, wish you were here to see my fancy red pajamas. Sure wish I had known
to take you some heavy pajamas last week so you could have them tonight. I know
you are going to freeze.

I hated it so bad that the car stalled where you could see it Monday night. I knew
how helpless you were feeling. You know darling, I was so used to depending
on you taking care of things that I was lazy. Guess it does me good to have to do
some things for myself. But I sure do miss you. I don't mind working or doing
anything I can if I could just be with you and have my arms around you and be able
to talk with you. I miss you so very much.

You may get to see the Christmas tree yet. It is still standing. The needles are
falling rather fast and furious. I just hate to take it down.

Darling, I have more than doubled up on my prayers – I've tripled. A dozen times
a day I take a minute to breathe a prayer. One of these days things will work

out. Please just keep up that faith and the Lord will take care of us. I love you, sweetheart, and as long as we have each other we can conquer anything.

I can't help wondering why this had to happen to us – but we can't question – we must just have faith.

Darling, I really think we ought to sell the house unfurnished. Even if we can't take the furniture with us, we can at least pick up some extra money by selling it. And since it looks like we aren't going to get our price for the house, I don't think we ought to let the furniture go too. We'll talk about it Sunday if I don't see you before.

Please don't talk about my forgiving you because from the first day you told me – you were forgiven and it is all forgotten. This is just a bad experience for us but I could very easily have been the one that caused it. I've done so many things wrong in my life but I just haven't had to go to jail over them. Please quit blaming yourself and hating yourself. I love you with all that is within me. You are my life and I'm not good without you. I need you, my dearest.

Honey, there are a lot of men in this world but I wouldn't swap my man for a million dollars. You're stuck with me for life.

All our love,
Joyce & Ron

P.S. I have tried to call Raby a couple of times but haven't gotten her. Will keep trying.

Wednesday
January 4, 1956

Hi Sweetheart,

1 o'clock
Baby, I guess I shouldn't write this letter because I'm sorta down but I guess I
have to feel like I'm talking to you. It's freezing cold up here and has been since
last night. We haven't had any mail since last Saturday. In general, the morale is
pretty low.

About all I can do is sit here and pray that I'll see some blinks tonight for
tomorrow. If it doesn't come tomorrow, do everything you can, short of making
Pruitt mad, in trying to get him to come up here. As I said before, we can't afford
to get him mad, but I sure would like to talk to him.

I wish that you could get some definite information because if this is going to go
on & on, I think you had better write for my retirement and push the house and try
to get someone to go to Jacksonville and get the Hudson and give it to the credit
union. I want you to have some cash in the bank. You might need it and I don't
know where it would come from without doing those things.

6:30
I was just standing in the window looking out. It is so cold and dreary looking out
there. Oh, how I wish I was with you. Baby, I need you more tonight than I have
ever needed you before. Darling, something must happen that we can be together.
Oh, how I love you.

I hate to think of you coming down tonight in the cold but since I have no way of
calling you, I know you'll be there.

7:30
Well, another Wednesday night and no signal. Honey, how much longer must this
go on? You know, I'm beginning to have harder feelings toward Pruitt than anyone
else. That man could come up here and tell me something if he weren't so lazy. I
can't understand why no one will come up here.

I got a big kick out of seeing you slinging Ron around tonight. I guess by the time I get out, he will be slinging you around.

Say, whenever I swing the match horizontal instead of up and down, that means that I don't know a thing and haven't had any word of why the delay, etc. I hope to get a letter from you tomorrow.

I wonder if it would do any good or if it would be bad for maybe you to talk to the judge about letting me out until he is ready to dispose of the deal. Looks like he could understand that I need to be supporting my family. This is just a thought. I guess you would have to talk it over with the preacher or Pruitt before even considering it.

I guess you think I'm impatient but you know, tomorrow will be 50 days. Darling, that's about like that many in years. Especially not knowing what the final outcome will be.

Well baby, keep smiling for both of us. Take good of yourself because you and that little boy are all that I have to hold on to.

Guess I'll close and say goodnight and God bless you. I love you. Hug Ron for me.

Love,
Bob

P.S. I take it from no blinks at all that you haven't heard a thing good. If you get a chance, call Kap and tell him to drop me a line.

Thursday
January 5, 1956

Hi Sweetheart,

8:30 AM
It's pretty early in the morning to be starting a letter that won't even be picked up until 9 tonight, but I just had to start writing. I got 4 letters from you this morning. Your Fri. – Sat. – Sun. – Mon. letters. Honey, I'm really getting a thrill out of them. The pictures are so good. The only thing is that I haven't gotten a good look at them for the tears. Everybody in the cellblock has seen them by now. They are passing them around like mad. Everybody says I have a beautiful wife and a handsome boy. Nobody knows that better than I do.

Gosh from your letter you must be working yourself to death. Mowing the lawn, washing clothes, washing the car, etc. I wish you wouldn't work so hard.

Honey, I sure am studying and enjoying the spiritual side of your letters. The things you say are wonderful and I sure need to hear them. I never realized before how much I need a little refill from day to day on the spiritual side. That's why I sure would like to see the preacher. I guess I'm paying for the many times I wouldn't go to church. Thank God for a good Christian wife who is helping me.

While I think of it, the next time you talk to Bobbie *(Stewart),* tell her that if she has written me every week, I haven't been getting them. I got a letter from her about the 2nd week I was here and the card from last week and that's all.

I'm afraid that the battery in the car is about to play out. The man out at Hi-Volt promised me that he would sell me his best one at a wholesale cost when I needed it. He is the owner and is a big man. I expect you had better go on and get one. You can tell him that I'm out of town and maybe he will give you a break on it. I would hate for you to get somewhere and get stuck without anyone to help you.

You know, I'm sure you don't notice it seeing him everyday but Ron is really growing and changing. He is really a beautiful little boy. I sure miss him and I'm afraid of what this time away will mean.

247

Sweetheart, what a time you must have had last month when the river didn't flow. I know that you must have been worried to death and frankly, I don't think if I had known that I would have survived at all. Right now I'm afraid that would have just about finished us up. Thank God that everything came out OK. I think you are mighty brave to carry it by yourself all that time.

I know that you and Ron have been cold there without the heaters fixed right. I declare it looks like that the very things that I should do for you all, I can't be there to do. It was sure cold here last night. I wouldn't be surprised if everyone has had pneumonia by the time we get out. The one thin blanket doesn't help much and the wind really whistles up there. We all sleep in our clothes.

Baby, I don't know if there is a thing to this hunch, but something that was said this morning may have something back of it, so do this. Call the jail and ask them if I have a bond set, or rather just call and ask how much my bond is. If by some chance there should be a bond and it is not too big, call Allied Bonding Company and ask for Wally Jefferson and he'll get me out. I can't explain all now but take a shot at it.

2:00 PM
Boy, what a day this is. I just got two more letters from you. The one you wrote Tuesday and the note about the insurance you wrote Wednesday.

I'm glad Rodgers came by to see you and also glad to hear of Art Deter's change of heart. You know, whether he has changed or not, I still say that he has more sense than most of the rest. I have often wished that I could talk to him.

You asked about the Orange Bowl Parade. Yes, we watched it both over TV and out the window. But, I would have liked to be there and see Ron watch the parade more than to see the parade itself.

You better tell Ron to keep his "fawnfee" out of cracks and that goes for other things, too. I'm glad to hear he is wearing his boots. I'm sure getting a kick out of the pictures.

Boy, I'm sure torn up about the insurance problem. You know, the original on the title for the Cadillac is at Central Bank. I don't know just how that will work out. It would seem to me that a general power of attorney would come near solving the whole thing. I'm not sure, you understand, that is just my opinion. I believe that if you come up here yourself, they would let me come out and sign that for you. You might either call them or just come on up and bulldog your way around.

The only reason that I can figure that the Grand Jury is holding on is to maybe bring the Bordeauxes into the picture. If you get a chance, you might go by and see them or something just to keep tabs, so if someone were to change their mind,

you would have a chance to speak up. I've heard that the Grand Jury can keep something like that as long as they want to.

5:30
Received your word about preacher. I'm sure I only got part of your message but the fellow was in a hurry. He was released. It's good to know that something is going on.

Honey, if you think of it, bring me another wash cloth. Someone took off with mine. I hope I won't need it for long but might as well have it.

Love to you both,
Bob

Friday
January 6, 1956

Hi Sweetheart,

Guess you won't get this until Monday. Gee, I wish that it didn't take so long for it to get to you. It seems to me like that the things I'm thinking now should get to you now.

Baby, it was wonderful to talk with you today. When the lawyer came for me to sign the papers they let me make the call. Guess it'll be 5 more weeks before I make another. It's funny, I go for days and can't contact you and then all of a sudden, two or three contacts in the same day.

Darling, just to hear your voice is wonderful. I don't think that the finest choir in the world could make such beautiful music.

While I was waiting outside, the preacher came up. He said he would call you and tell you what he told me, which was not much. He hadn't heard anything. He did seem a little concerned about old man Morrison. Said that he threatened to shoot me. I wouldn't be surprised if the old fool wouldn't try it.

If I do get everything worked out, I'll probably have to watch my step leaving the courtroom. I told the preacher to tell Pruitt. Don't know as there is much he can do though. However, I'll worry about that when the time comes.

I got a letter from Brownie today. He said that he has been going to lots of fires, etc. not too much news, about like you would expect Brownie to write.

You would get a big kick out of some of the things that happen up here. Can you imagine a bunch of grown men trying to hide a roll of toilet paper like a squirrel so you can have some all week? Or getting a cake of soap and trying not to let anybody know you've got it so that it will last? It really is funny and ridiculous at the same time but that's living in jail.

I sure hope that by the time you get this we will have some definite news and maybe things will begin to move.

Honey, I could hardly talk to the preacher today. I don't know what is the matter with me. I get tears in my eyes over almost nothing. It makes me so mad, I don't know what to do. Guess I'm reverting to my childhood.

I wanted to be able to talk to him alone and not through the cage. You know they let the Catholics go into a room to talk to the priests, but not us. I sure wanted to pray with him a little. He couldn't talk to me like I wanted him to. You know a little spiritual guidance from a man like him could mean so much.

I'm sure going to be a church-going boy when I get out. I've rediscovered that I need to sit down and listen to the Lord a lot more.

7:30
Darling, what a lift I get when I look down and see you and Ron down there. I could tell that he was playing games. I'm so anxious to be able to play with him again and to see what new things he knows.

Darling, you are a wonderful mother to him. When he grows up, he'll be so proud of you because you are not only a good mother but a beautiful one.

Honey, I don't know anything special to write. I'll see you before you get this, I hope. I love you a thousand times. I love you.

Love to you both,
Bob

Saturday
January 7, 1956

Hello Sweetheart,

Noon
Thought I'd start your letter darling. You know, I sit around and I begin to think of you and I guess I couldn't stand it if I didn't start writing to you. Honey, I sure thought we would be together today. I sorta had a feeling. But I guess, as usual, my hunches are always wrong these days.

It is cold up here again today and the wind is whistling. I was just standing here looking out the window wondering what you and Ron are doing. I sure hate these Saturdays.

Honey, you know I'm about convinced that if I'm going to out of here in the foreseeable future, it will be through the efforts of the preacher getting the Grand Jury to turn the thing loose. I know that he works on it when he can. But when you get a chance, call him just to sorta keep the ball rolling. I can't understand why the man didn't call him back Friday.

I'm sitting out in the bull-pen writing and looking at Big Top on TV. There are some cute dogs on. I hope maybe Ron is looking at them.

You know, I wish I could somehow get my files up here so I could get my income tax off. We could use the money.

4:00 PM
I'm getting sorta stinky or that is, more stinky. The hot water has been on the fritz for a couple of days. It always picks the cold weather to act up.

I was just thinking that if the Grand Jury turns the deal loose on Monday and the court couldn't get ready for the new trial, maybe they will finish the old one and let me out till Thursday for the other one. I sure would like to spend some time with you before I leave.

We are waiting for our macaroni and water for supper. I think that's what the deal is for tonight. "Oh goody." Ha! I got fooled, we had minced ham and tea. So I had my usual bread and tea. Boy! Would I love to have a steak on the grill in the backyard with one of your delicious potatoes and salad with a piece of chocolate ice box pie. The water drops on the page are drippings from my mouth. After all, I've got the best cook in the world for a wife. In fact, I'm sold on that sweet gal I married. In fact, I love you!

7:30
Well, what a surprise. A blink tonight. I can't imagine what you have heard unless it is a good word from the preacher. I sure hope so.

You know, it's a funny thing. I had prayed that there may be a blink tonight so I know my prayers are getting through.

Guess I'll close. Hug Ron for me. I love you.

Bob

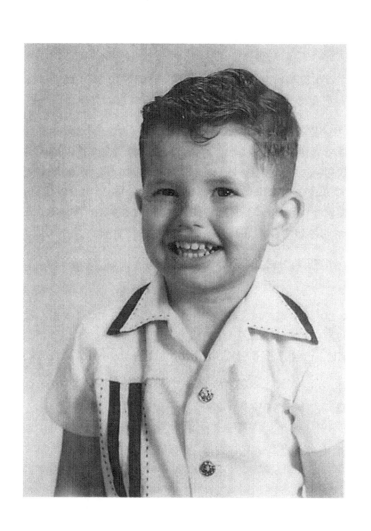

Sunday
January 8, 1956

Hello Sweetheart,

6:00 PM
Gee baby, you have been gone 4 hours and it seems to me like 4 years. Darling, I love you so much and to see you means so much to me.

Gosh honey, I think it's getting colder and colder. The new pajamas are real nice and I'm having to fight to hold on to them. I see you bought a new T-shirt. You shouldn't have. One of the old ones would have been OK. I don't want you to spend anything on me that isn't absolutely necessary. I so want you and Ron to have everything that you need and I know that money is scarce. Anyway, I appreciate it just like I appreciate anything that you do.

Baby, I sure wish that I had thought to tell you not to come tonight. I know it will be cold.

I have said this so many times before that I hesitate to say it again, but I must live in hope. This letter, I guess, will get to you Tuesday. I just hope I'm there by the time it is. Darling, I sure hope that this time will be the finish. I'm mighty tired of this place.

Honey, this deal about the house makes me sick. If $2,000 over what we owe is all we can get, I guess that's it. If we could just hold off for a while, maybe we could get more. But I'm sure we haven't a chance unless I could get out right away and get to work and make enough to get by on for a month or two. I feel like the season should bring a better price. I'm in agreement with you that we certainly wouldn't sell it at that price furnished.

I love you, my dear, a thousand times, I love you. Keep on being my sweet darling. Kiss Ron for me.

Love,
Bob

Monday
January 9, 1956

Hello Sweetheart,

2:30
I just know, darling, that I'll beat this letter there but I feel like I want to write it anyhow just to feel near you.

Gee baby, I hope I'm not riding too high on my hopes but I just have faith enough to believe that it is about over.

I just wrote a note to Bobbie and Raby. I didn't say anything about any anticipated date.

Darling, I want to be with you so much that I could almost fly out of here.

Say baby, those pajamas are really wonderful. I know that I would have frozen to death last night and today without them. I just hate to have to wear something nice in this place.

I know that you and Ron must have frozen to death last night. Boy, it was cold.

I have been waiting all day hoping that the mailman would come, but nothing yet.

According to my calculations, I saw two blinks so I hope I'll see you tomorrow. Baby, I sure hope so. It will be the answer to a mighty wonderful lot of prayers.

Darling, even if I'm out, I still want to get this on paper. You can look for your husband to be a better Christian than you ever imagined possible. That is, through the help of the Lord, I will be.

I love you so much and hope I can spend a little time with you. If I do get out Tuesday and have to go on, this will get to you Wednesday. I want us to redouble our efforts to liquidate the house so we can be together forever.

Guess I'll close and hope this is the last letter I'll ever have to write to you from behind bars.

God bless you, dear, and remember, I love you.

Bob

SEVEN.

G*uess I'll close and hope this is the last letter I'll ever have to write to you from behind bars."*

On Tuesday, January 10th, 1956, he got his wish and his day in court. That may have been the last letter written from behind bars, however, it was not the last letter from this time of separation. Less than a month later, he was living in Charleston, SC, while my mother and I remained in Miami as she continued to try to sell our home.

One hundred letters were exchanged between my parents during the eight weeks he was in jail. There was also one letter, tucked inside of another, written to me. There were six newspaper clippings of articles included that helped me to better understand the progression of events. And yet, there are still so many unanswered questions.

Several of the cards and notes from their friends mentioned in the letters were saved in the box. And, as I looked through family photos, I found the photo of me, in front of a sad looking Christmas tree with my gifts, including the record player and cowboy boots so often discussed in the letters. I always assumed that my dad, the amateur photographer, snapped the photo. But now I know that he would not have been able to, since he was in jail that Christmas. The same goes for the photo of my mother and me, along with the Flynns, watching the Orange Bowl Parade. And the photo of my third birthday party at the Flynn home. These innocent photos are now more precious to me than ever before.

With my frustration growing, I finally asked my attorney to help me to obtain the legal documents from the Miami court system during that time. He was able to speak with an Assistant State Attorney and Public Records Custodian in Miami. By phone, she didn't give him much hope for records that far back, but said she would look into it immediately. She was true to her word, and shortly sent an official reply that they were unable to find any records. I have since been told there had been a flooded basement at one time and the records from the 1940s and 1950s were lost.

I also contacted the Dade County Public Library requesting any newspaper clippings they might have. They were very willing to help, but, unfortunately, only located two articles, one of which I already had from my box of letters.

I continued to search online for the past friends mentioned in the letters. Those that were my parents age and older have long since passed away. Their children who might have had some knowledge of the events are also gone. I struck out trying to find any Boy Scouts from that time, especially only knowing a few of the names to search for. My cousin, who was the victim, as well as most of our family members, are no longer with us. Another dead end.

I came to the conclusion that it was time to pull the story together using the letters, photographs, newspaper articles, and limited personal knowledge from remaining family and friends. It was time for me to accept that I will never have the opportunity to know everything that went on during that time. And yet, I am amazed at how much of the story was left for me in that box of letters. Any additional information that I was able to uncover was just a bonus.

EIGHT.

For many years, even dating back to before they married, my father served as the Scoutmaster for Troop One at Central Baptist Church. His good friend, Guy Cutulo, was the assistant Scoutmaster. At the time, my father was one of the youngest Scoutmasters, and Troop One was one of the largest troops, in Florida. It has been long since disbanded.

My father was successful, and often awarded, for his leadership. In fact, he was given the highest award that a local Scout Council can bestow on an adult leader: the Silver Beaver award. This pewter beaver, attached to a blue and white striped ribbon to be worn around the neck, was given to him in recognition of distinguished service in scouting.

In one of the newspaper articles, Guy Cutulo is listed as the physical education teacher at Citrus Grove Elementary and Junior High School. My dad was listed as an insurance salesman. However, both men were unemployed after their arrests. A family friend, Cecil Carroll, was the agency vice-president of Independent Life and Accident Insurance Company, and gave my dad a second chance by letting him resume his career, in another state, once the verdict was reached.

In an article from the *Miami Herald* newspaper, dated December 7, 1955, it states that, "York pleaded guilty before Judge Willard on Nov. 1, on charges of making improper advances to a 13-year-old boy last year. The court withheld sentence and ordered York to leave Florida with his family."

It goes on to say, "He complied with that order, only to be arrested at Jacksonville on the way to a new home and insurance job in South Carolina. The arrest followed the complaint of the boy's father, made to Peace Justice Francis J. Christie."

I know for a fact that the complaint that caused my father to be re-arrested and brought back to Miami was filed by my uncle, Buddy, on behalf of his 13-year-old son, my cousin Robert. I can only assume that he was also the source of the original charge the previous year. There are numerous mentions of how upset, and understandably so, my uncle was with my father, even to the point that he, along with his father, "Old Man Morrison," threatened my father's life. I can't imagine him being happy with my father simply being told to leave the state of Florida for his punishment.

I don't know any details regarding the first trial. The letters and most of the articles I have seen, stem from the second arrest, when my father found himself in jail for eight weeks. Therefore, this story picks up after an initial arrest, charge, and trial that resulted in the outcome of a suspended sentence, "on condition that York leave the state and never return."

According to one of the articles, Cutulo was charged with three counts of lewd and lascivious conduct for sexually assaulting a minor under fourteen years of age. One similar charge was filed against my dad. One article states that there were other offenses, but the statute of limitations had run out. They went on to say that the offenses involved seven boys, who at the time were 13 years old. It also pointed out that several of the boys were members of prominent Miami families. One article states "Arthur E. Huttoe, chief prosecutor for Court of Crimes, said the acts took place over a period of several years in Miami, and on trips on which the two men took the boys." What isn't clear, is exactly what the offenses were that were charged against each man. Was my father responsible for more than the one charge for which he accepted guilt?

Sensational headlines such as "Molester Trial" and "Boy Fondler," designed to draw you in, caused my stomach to turn. This was not my father. This couldn't be the dad I loved and that I know loved me. And yet, he pleaded guilty. My father pleaded guilty, and became the first person in Dade County to be handled locally under the legislature's sexual psychopath statute. The article went on to say that, should he be judged a criminal sexual psychopath, "he could be committed to the Chattahoochee State Hospital for treatment."

A *Miami Herald* article from November 18, 1955, with the headline "Psychiatric Test Ordered for Accused Molester" adds this: "Also charged with three offenses involving boys of the same troop, Guy Cutulo, 38, suspended Citrus Grove physical education instructor, Thursday pleaded innocent and demanded a jury trial in Judge Willard's court, set for Dec. 5-7." It concluded with, "Cutulo is free under $3,000 bond."

From the various sources, it appears Cutulo was to have three separate trials. One occurred in December, 1955, but the others happened in the following year. The one mystery I haven't been able to solve is what his final outcome might have been.

I was able to speak with Cutulo's nephew. His dad, Vincent, was Guy's older brother, as well as our family barber. He told me that Guy's situation was rarely talked about in their family. He was not aware of the three trials, but didn't think Guy served any time.

A followup article states that my father was not deemed to be considered a "criminal sexual psychopath" under the new child molester law. However, the two court-appointed psychiatrists concluded in their reports that my father was a "sex deviate" but revealed "no mental disorder coupled with criminal propensities toward commission of sexual offenses."

MEETING NIGHT
FRIDAY 7:30

PHONES 834897
38673

TROOP ONE

BOY SCOUTS OF AMERICA

ROBERT L. YORK
SCOUTMASTER

CENTRAL BAPTIST CHURCH
500 N.E. 1ST AVENUE
MIAMI, FLA.

Boy Fondler Is Ruled No Psychopath

Two Miami psychiatrists held Monday that Robert L. York, 35, insurance salesman and longtime Boy Scout leader, cannot be considered a "criminal sexual psychopath" un___ ___rid__'s new child molest___

In their ___ cult Judge ___ said their ___ tions show ___ nor unnatu___

Judge ___ dered Yor___ Judge Ber___ inal Cour___ ed senten___ to leave I___ of guilty ___ old boy la___

York's c___ attention when the boy's ___ filed a peace justice charge and had York re-arrested as he reached Jacksonville. In jail since his return to Miami, York became the first person in Dade County to undergo psychiatric tests under the new law.

If he had been found to be a sexual psychopath, he could have been committed to the state mental hospital for treatment. When released, under the law, he could not have been sentenced or prosecuted further for the 1954 offense.

York is to face Judge Willard for the second time probably Thursday.

York is married and the father of a 3-year-old boy. He resided formerly at 3050 NW 15th St.

Molester Trial Is Set By Willard

Criminal Court Judge Ben C. Willard today set trial date for one accused child molester and ordered another man charged with a similar offense picked up and examined by psychiatrists.

Guy Cutolo, 38, a former physical education teacher at Citrus Grove Elementary School, entered pleas of innocence to three counts charging lewd, lascivious or indecent assault on a minor and asked for a jury trial. The

First Test Of Sex Law Due Here

Dade county's first test of a new Florida law covering child molesters and other sexual psychopaths was put in motion Tuesday by Circuit Judge J. Fritz Gordon.

On a petition filed by State Attorney George A. Brautigam, the judge appointed two Miami psychiatrists — Dr. James L. And-

2 Men Face Morals Charges After Check On Boy's Story

Two leaders of a group of Miami boys were charged today with engaging in unnatural sex acts with the youngsters.

They were identified as Guy Cutolo, 38, a physical education teacher at the Citrus Grove Elementary and Junior High school at 2134 NW 5th St., and Robert L. York, 35, of 3050 NW

15th St., who is unemployed.

Arthur E. Huttoe, chief prosecutor for Court of Crimes, said the acts took place over a period of several years in Miami and on trips on which the two men took the boys.

Boy Tells Parents

The charges were filed by Huttoe after one of the boys told

his parents of the practices.

Cutolo was charged with three counts of lewd and lascivious conduct by assaulting a minor under 14 years of age, and one similar charge was filed against York.

Huttoe said many other acts with which the men could have been charged took place more than two years ago, and therefore could not be prosecuted because of the statute of limitations.

All of the offenses involved seven boys who at the time were 13 years old, Huttoe said. The prosecutor said several of the boys were members of prominent Miami families.

York Arraignment Set

York, Huttoe said, will be arraigned tomorrow in Criminal Court, Cutolo's arraignment will take place later.

The investigation which resulted in the arrest of the two men was made over a period of several weeks by Detective R. E. Gibson of the Miami Police Juvenile Bureau.

W. R. Thomas, Dade County superintendent of education, said Cutolo was suspended today from his teaching duties. Thomas said he could take no official action toward the teacher until he has a copy of the warrant and discussed the matter with the School Board.

concluded, the panels provided ___ring to put the costume with___dinance.

Guilty Plea Nets Exile

Robert L. York, 35, of 3050 NW 15th St., today pleaded guilty to lewd and lascivious behavior with a boy under 14 years of age and Criminal Court Judge Ben C. Willard immediately suspended sentence on condition that York leave the state and never return.

York and Guy Cutolo, 38, a former physical education instructor at Citrus Grove Elemen-

Boy Scouts of America Silver Beaver Award

NINE.

Does this change the life I knew with the father I loved? Do I now judge my father by the hideous crime committed more than 60 years ago? In one word, no. And yet, now that I know, how do I come to terms with this new found knowledge? First of all, I have to believe it was intended that one day I would know this story. To keep a box of incriminating letters and articles has to mean you understand the risk of having them found. Even if my mother had held on to them without my dad's knowledge, the fact that I know that they were moved after her death from her closet to the tool shed, suggests he was aware of them and the possibility that they could be found. If he did not want them to ever see the light of day, then why not destroy them?

I would never want someone to think I'm comparing my situation to theirs in the loss of a loved one. I know that this was not an actual death. And yet, for me, it is the death of my father's image, or the father I thought I knew. So, whether I like it or not, I find myself in the five stages of grief, starting with denial.

I admit to being shocked at first, almost disbelieving in what I found, although there it was in black and white. Yes, there was a feeling of loss, even if it was just the loss of how I once perceived my father.

Second comes anger. Yes, I am angry that this ever happened. Angry at what my mother had to endure. And angry for the pain and suffering the boys and their families felt from my father's actions. I'm also angry that I never had the chance to know my aunt, uncle, and cousins. It makes me angry that my father never felt he could tell me, although I'm sure there was always the fear that someone might confide in me. If there had been a time to tell me, it would have been after my mother passed away. As an adult, I would like to think that I could have handled it. Plus, it would have opened the door for me to tell him how I felt, as someone who had been sexually molested as a child.

But then, I also feel angry at myself for thinking I deserved to hear the truth from him. This was his story to share or to keep to himself. Plus, our relationship had become much stronger after my mother's passing, and he must have felt something of this magnitude would surely have changed that.

The next stage is bargaining. Do I wish I didn't know? No. Do I wish that I had questioned my parents more, regarding the separation from my relatives? Yes, something was clearly wrong, and my parents' excuse of "just not getting along," was lame. Yet, I chose to accept it, when discussing it might have brought things into the open, and allow for healing. But bargaining tends to keep things in the past, and it does no good for me to think, "If only." I need to focus on the present.

Then comes depression. I can admit that this revelation has taken its toll on my emotions. One minute I think I've made peace with it, and the next, I can't stop the tears from flowing. I go from thinking like an outsider reading a book or researching a paper, to the realization that this is my life. I am one of those sexually assaulted young boys. Not by my father or his friend, Guy, but in the same scenario just a few years later. I don't think of myself as a victim. I don't want to be a victim. And yet, as I read the letters and newspaper clippings, I know that I am a part of the story, too.

The final stage is acceptance. Am I there yet? Can I accept the truth about my father's past sins? Can I accept what this did to my mother? And more importantly, can I accept what he was accused of doing to my cousin when I know, first hand, of the confusion that sexual advances by an adult can cause a child? I realize that acceptance does not mean all is forgiven. It doesn't mean everything is all right. But by achieving some form of acceptance, hopefully I can move on. After all, it was over 60 years ago. I was young, and have no memory of his crime being a part of my life, other than the loss of one set of relatives, and the move to Tennessee. Do I condone his actions? Of course not. Do I accept the fact that he made a terrible mistake and yet was still a loving, caring father to me? Yes.

TEN.

My father was finally released from the Dade County jail that second week of January in 1956, and headed north once again to Charleston, SC. For the next three-plus months, he wrote to my mother every day, sometimes two to three letters daily. I am left with more than 100 of his letters to my mom written from Charleston. Unfortunately, I do not have her reply letters. To be honest, I didn't expect much additional information from this group of letters, but quickly saw that I was wrong.

The first letter was written on Sunday afternoon, February 5th, 1956. He begins by saying that it seems they are spending half of their lives communicating by mail, and how sick he is of this situation. He then brings her up to date since his arrival on Friday, when he flew into Jacksonville in a sixty passenger plane with only four other passengers. He checked his baggage at the bus station, and after learning that Cecil Carroll had a luncheon meeting, he began to work on his old Hudson. It had been stored in the Carroll's garage since his arrest in November, and was now in need of a new heater hose.

When Cecil was free to talk, he told my dad that he wanted him to go to Charleston for two weeks, and then on to Conway. He thought that after that time, he might be able to place him permanently, giving him a manager's job, "if the deal in Miami hadn't bounced up again." He feared it would put both of them in a tight spot if "things down there blew up again." My dad told him that he had to clear $100 a week or he would have to return to Miami and figure something out there. This was my first indication that the verdict had not left him "exiled" from Florida, as with the previous charge.

He left Jacksonville Sunday morning, driving through rain, and arrived in Charleston around three in the afternoon. After looking at about a dozen places, he found a room in a boarding house for $15 a week. He wrote that he had already spotted First Baptist Church, and planned to go over after he got a bite to eat.

He continued with "Honey, I like not to have made it thru the daily Bible reading last night without you to do some of the reading, and when I knelt to pray, I left a crook in my arm for you to fit in."

I read through this set of my father's letters from beginning to end, and found several things that were different from the set of letters which he had written to her from jail. On the humorous, and yet annoying, side, he seemed to have picked up the word "kid" to address my mother, instead of "honey" or "baby", as he always had before. On the uncomfortable side of things, the sweet flirting that he had written in his letters from jail, was now much more sexual. Of course, he had known that the jail letters were being read, coming and going, and thus, he may have been more cautious with what he wrote in those. However, this set of letters started out with longing and escalated into a somewhat more direct, and even lewd, sexual approach.

The other thing that struck me was the desperate need to be in church. Like an alcoholic in need of an AA meeting, he searched for just the right church and went as often as the doors were open.

After all of the missed holidays while he was in jail, my parents were now coming up on Valentine's Day, and once again, they were not together. Finances were so tight that travel was not an option. The house had still not sold, and the income tax refund had not arrived. The letters expressed a desperation when they thought that they had a buyer for the house and were then let down. A new realtor took over, the price came down, and they went back and forth on whether to include the furniture or not. And then, every day they were thinking that the income tax refund would arrive and be a quick band-aid for a much more serious problem.

My mother continued to work, and I stayed in nursery school. Not having her set of letters, I don't know her day to day routine, but imagine that it had not changed since he had gotten out of jail. His letters to her offered encouragement, knowing everything she was going through.

As I said, he was writing up to three letters daily. He was fixated on the mail and what time it had to go into the box to make pickup so that it could arrive the next day in Miami. He started his letters in the morning and then finished them standing in the post office, writing at the table to make sure it got out on time. He convinced my mother to get a PO box so she would have his letters sooner.

Eventually he began to become a little more settled in Charleston. He hadn't been a fan at first, but soon started to appreciate the city, and feel that they could be happy there. Coming from the Miami office, he was clearly more experienced than many of the men with whom he worked, and in time found some success.

Debit life insurance involves basically selling insurance to lower income families and collecting premiums on a weekly basis. Usually the agent has to go door to door to collect payments. My dad was used to the easy-to-walk street grid system of Miami but had to adapt in Charleston, since the "debits" were not close to each other. This caused him to drive out from town and park his car to walk the "debit" door to door for several miles. His boss was trying to convince him to stay in Charleston and not move on as first expected.

During his free time, he would check out the different areas of town, and available homes for rent. The going price seemed to be around $85 a month, sometimes furnished, and sometimes not, depending on the area. He came close to committing to a place a couple of times, but then decided he needed my mother's input. He knew already that she wouldn't be happy about having to move there. Plus, he needed to get a commitment from Cecil that he would continue to have a job there, before signing a lease.

He mentioned in several letters how nice the people in Charleston were, and how they would speak to you as they passed you on the street. Then as spring arrived, he was amazed by the beautiful flowers and gardens.

When not at work, church, or writing letters in the post office, he could be found playing canasta with his 45-year-old landlady, Lola, and two other women at the boarding house, one 60 and the other 75, whom he referred to as "the girls." They took him on a sightseeing tour, but he remarked that Lola drove down the center of the road, so he spent more time watching for cars than the scenery.

Without my mother's letters, I don't know much about the antics of the Flynn family, Bud and Kat Stone, or my mother's parents, during that time. There were several mentions of Raby and the need to write to her, and check on her, as well as the fact that they still owed her money. However, Monnie "Brownie" Flynn finally proposed to his girlfriend, Elaine, and they set a wedding date. My dad wanted to be there, but also wanted to be with us for Easter. There was concern about his getting away from work twice, and the expense of flying or going by train or bus. The Hudson was constantly in need of repair, and not reliable for such a long trip.

Dad sent my mother church bulletins and told her about prayer meetings. He mentioned a church Boy Scout Troop and their need for volunteers. Fortunately, *(and much to my relief)*, he also said how sad it was that he had messed up so badly that he could never help the Scouts again. After trying several churches, my dad found a home in the Ashley River Baptist Church. It seemed to have more couples his age and he became more and more involved.

On February 17th, he splurged and paid 50 cents to go the movie. He saw Jimmy Stewart in *The Stratton Story* with June Allyson. It was based on the story of major league pitcher, Monty Stratton, who lost his leg and went into the depths of depression. His wife stood by him, and with her help, and a prosthetic leg, he eventually worked his way back into the minor leagues. My dad shared that he sort of felt the same way as Monty Stratton had, and, because of my mother's strength and forgiveness, that he, too, would come back.

The first mention of my uncle Buddy came in a letter written on February 20th. After mentioning their lawyer Pruitt, he wrote, "Speaking of Pruitt etc., I imagine that the time Buddy would try to stir up something will be after you leave as then he would probably get the idea that we were gone for good. I somehow have enough faith to believe that it would avail him nothing."

In the February 27th letter, he offered up a plan: Since the house had still not sold, and the income tax refund had yet to arrive, he would come back to Miami to work, get out of debt, and then they would move away. He said "Now, I know that this has lots of ramifications to this and so much would depend on whether Buddy would let me alone or not. I, of course, would want to talk to Pruitt about this."

He continued in another paragraph, "Although I'm firmly convinced that if it is the thing to do that the Lord will help us. I'd say that the biggest unknown factor in the Miami deal is Buddy."

Ashley River Baptist Church

Savannah Highway at Albemarle Drive
CHARLESTON, S. C.

Thirteen
Glorious Years

FIRST AUDITORIUM

PRESENT AUDITORIUM WITH A PORTION OF THE EDUCATIONAL BUILDING

SUNDAY, APRIL 15, 1956   ROBERT W. MAJOR, PASTOR

Ashley River Baptist Church program, Charleston, 1956

ELEVEN.

My dad was able to come back to Miami for the first weekend in March. He wrote my mother as soon as he returned to Charleston, "Honey, I can still see you, when I shut my eyes, standing there waving and you looked pretty as a picture."

I don't think it was a perfect weekend since he wrote, "Honey, don't worry about last night. I know that everybody has to blow off some steam sometimes and I know that you certainly have had enough to really get you up in the air. I'm just glad I was there so we could talk about it. Maybe that helped a little. I hope so."

I have wondered if my mother ever reached a point of total frustration with what his actions had done to our lives. With his non-stop letter writing and need to be in church every chance, along with the nightly phone calls, my father had a desperate air about him. He would call two or three times a night trying to get hold of my mother. There were times that the line was busy and he would give up or the operator would tell him there was trouble on the line. But my mother, with a three-year-old child, would appear to not be home some evenings until late. Or she may have reached the point at times, understandably, that she just didn't want to talk to him.

People continued to look at the house, and both of my parents were wishing and hoping a deal could be made. But they had no luck, and still no income tax refund when his March 7th letter arrived.

Another article regarding the arrests and trial had come out in the paper, and my mother mailed it to him. His response was, "I read the article you sent. It gives me cold chills to read anything for fear they might get the stink stirred up again. I have thought since I left that I wish I had called Guy and advised him to take the prosecution's offer. I'm afraid it won't help any if his trial kicks up a stink. I may write him to that effect not mentioning my own interest. What do you think?"

On the 17th he wrote, "I hate to hear about that other case coming up before Guy's. We need to do a little praying for him." I don't know what or whose case they were talking about, other than one story that he shared with me. My dad's step-mother had told his younger half-sister that there were actually three men from the Scout troop involved. However, the newspaper articles never mentioned anyone other than my dad and Guy. And this was the only mention in the letters between my parents that there might be a third man involved. In a letter Guy wrote to my father 11 years earlier, when in the Navy and stationed in the Philippines, Guy said "But, honestly, I do miss all the good times the 3 of us had and all my brownies *(Young Scouts)*."

During this time, each letter had some mention of church. Either a service, revival, or a church program was folded and included with a letter. Stories about work and the men he worked with became more regular, and there were boarding house stories such as the landlady inviting him down for breakfast one morning. She served him hot apple juice, and he later commented in his letter to my mom that he was not a fan.

The house had still not sold and there was no sign of the income tax refund. My father went to a local bank and applied for a loan. Of course, they needed the money but if he was staying in Charleston, then he wanted to establish credit. He mentioned that they were going to write the credit bureau in Miami, and he asked my mother to call a friend there and ask her to try to make it good.

He said, "You might remind her that the conviction has been wiped out, if they are like the insurance company and make a record of it. I sure hope it goes OK without a hitch as it will be embarrassing if not." This was the only mention of the charges being dropped, or as he said, "wiped out." This also explained to me why and how he was free to return to Miami.

There was a constant fear that someone would find out about his past. He mentioned later that it would be just his luck that the folks in Miami tell the Charleston bank, and that the woman he was working with there probably went to the same church. And in one letter, he mentioned one of the supervisors from Independent Life coming to town and how he was sure that he knew his story and wondered if he would tell. He then rationalized that with Cecil Carroll in his corner, no one at the company would want to cross him. Still, I had to wonder how many times through the decades there had been a fear of word getting out – or worse, someone telling me.

I had to laugh when I read what he wrote about the flowers in bloom all over Charleston. Many years ago, he and I, after my mother passed away, decided to add a florist to our Christmas store, the Mistletoe Shop. The son of some dear friends was getting married. They asked me to do the flowers and it seemed like a natural progression to add a florist to our business. My choice of names for the business was "Blooming Idiot." However, we finally decided on something less dramatic, "Blooming Colours."

In his March 10th letter, my dad wrote, "The azaleas are really beautiful. But I've got the sweetest flower in the world in Miami. In fact, two of them. A rose and a little bud. Of course, you know you have a flower up here too. <u>A Blooming Idiot</u>."

Often in churches, a Sunday School class might be named after someone, either biblical or not. It seemed there was a Training Union class at Central Baptist in Miami that was named after my father. In one letter he wondered, if after everything that happened, they had renamed that class. I never learned the answer but can't imagine that they would not have made a name change.

Finally, hallelujah! The income tax refund arrived March 11th, 1956. This let them see a light at the end of a long dark tunnel. My father had settled in at work and was quickly becoming the highest producer. He was able to send money back to Miami and my mother was able to continue paying their creditors.

At one point, before the weekly check arrived, they were past due on everything. And to top it all off, Independent Life made a mistake in my dad's check, deducting more than they were supposed to. He had a fit, but the best the company could do was correct it in the next week's check. My mother was out of money and my dad was begging her, in his letter, to ask a friend to help and tell them that they would pay them back within the week when the other check arrived. I can't even imagine the stress put on her and how she coped.

Now that there was a little breathing room financially, my dad took in a couple more movies. He saw *"Helen of Troy"* and the Lillian Roth Story, *"I'll Cry Tomorrow"* starring Susan Hayward.

My dad learned that Dr. Angell, aka "Preacher," was going to come up from Miami and lead a revival in Spartanburg. He wanted desperately to slip away and attend. He felt he needed to see "his" preacher. Cecil Carroll was going to be in Columbia and my dad asked him if he'd like to ride along. He met Cecil at the Hotel Jefferson, where he was staying. My dad didn't think he could spend the $6.00 a night there, so he stayed at the Davis Hotel for $3.50.

Cecil bought his breakfast the next morning and had the company buy his lunch. My dad was very grateful. They talked about my dad's future, and Cecil mentioned that he could give him the manager's job in Greenwood. But by now, my dad had become comfortable in Charleston, familiar with the city, had found a church, and was beginning to make some decent money. So Greenwood didn't interest him at all.

It turned out Cecil wasn't able to go to Spartanburg for the revival. So my dad, leaving later than anticipated, headed out. He arrived just as the choir was walking in.

He wrote: "Honey, the preacher sounded like he knew I was there from what he preached. He talked about how Christ can sometimes step in and make us suffer just to get our lives straightened out. He said so many things that really hit me. When they gave the invitation, he kept stressing on rededicating our lives until I found myself going down the aisle. Dr. Angell didn't even see me then. And when the man called out the names (there were two for membership, one for baptism and me) the preacher was sitting on the platform with his head sorta in his hand. When they called my name, his arm fell down and his head jerked up and you never saw such an expression as he had. He seemed tickled to see me."

Unfortunately, they only got to talk for a few minutes because Dr. Angell was headed out with "some people." But, my father concluded, "It really did me lots of good to hear Dr. Angell and meant lots to me to have the chance to rededicate my life in the church."

Mom and Dad discussed Easter, and wanting to be together then. He encouraged my mom to go buy a new dress but she ended up making her Easter dress. She sent him a fabric swatch and the ladies at the boarding house helped him pick out jewelry. He asked her to have his white pants cleaned. He said that they had been tight the previous year, but should fit this year, as he was having most of his pants taken in from weight loss.

He did come back to Miami for Easter weekend. When he returned to Charleston, he wrote and apologized for the times he didn't go to church and the times he made my mother feel guilty for going on without him. He got back to Charleston Easter Sunday afternoon and rushed to Ashley River Baptist for the evening service. He said that he asked the Lord to forgive him for another of his many sins and hopes that my mother will, too.

Tucked inside one of the letters were two photos from that Easter. My dad admitted they weren't very good, and I have to agree. No one looks happy, but there I am with my mouth open wide standing next to a large stuffed bunny that he had found on sale and brought with him from Charleston.

He said in that letter: "I don't guess you ever stopped to think about it, but you know, I feel like you and Ron are the only two people in all this world who I can feel completely love me. I know that there may be others who have sympathy and who maybe think kindly of me because of you, but I really feel that not even Daddy has the same sort of love that he once had. So you can see that I need you so very much, because of your love, forgiveness and understanding."

The house had still not sold. The new Education Director at church expressed interest, then there were the "Spanish family" and the "Italian Folks." But none of them made an offer to buy the house.

Easter, Miami, 1956

TWELVE.

On Wednesday evening, April 4th, my parents talked by phone. He then began a letter by apologizing. "I'm just sorry that we had to spend part of the time talking about unpleasant things. By the way, after talking with you, by the time I got to the house, I just decided that I wouldn't sleep good until I talked to Guy. So I called him and told him in no uncertain terms that he had better get right with his lawyer about the statements that they sent into the newspaper and that if he didn't, that if I was dragged back down there because of them, that the court and the public was going to find out with whom the investigation started and that I positively wouldn't stand for anymore such statements. He claimed, of course, that he knew nothing of it and that it was the prosecutor, O'Dwyer, who made the statements, etc. Anyhow, I got it off my chest and thought that it would be better than writing it as I didn't want to put anything in writing. Anyway, I'm not going to lose any sleep on it as I just feel like the good Lord will take care of us."

After my dad talked with Guy, it seems that Guy turned around and called my mother. Once my dad learned of this, he wrote, "I was really burned up that Guy called you back after I called him. I sorta thought after I had hung up from calling him that I should have told him not to call you. If he ever calls you again, and I hope he doesn't, and starts blowing off about coming over to our house being a bad influence on him, you might remind him that six or seven years ago, I went out in the Gables and got him out of a mess, and if he doesn't believe that it was me that got him out, you can tell him to ask the lawyers, Bill Gray and Rex Hawkins, if they didn't drop the deal because I asked them to. Also, you can remind him that when that happened, his scouting registration was cancelled and that he couldn't have worked with any scout troop if I hadn't stuck my nose out trying to help him." He concluded with, "I just wish I was there for about an hour, I could shut him up forever."

In researching Guy J. Cutulo, his name pops up on a list of Scoutmasters for Troop 7, in Coral Gables, Florida. He is listed as being their Scoutmaster from 1948-1949, the same time my father refers to going "out in the Gables" to get "him out of a mess." Apparently it was my dad who persuaded the attorneys to "drop the deal," as well as getting his scouting registration reinstated. I assume that he then returned to Troop One, as assistant Scoutmaster, alongside my dad.

Clearly Guy had been in this sort of trouble before, and as much as I didn't want to believe it, since he was a long time friend of my father, I have to wonder at what point my father decided to join in? Also, if my dad had not brought Guy back into the fold with Troop One, maybe the situation with my cousin might not have happened.

On April 6th, my granddad Broadway, my mother's father, had a heart attack. There was concern but he seemed to be resting and they expected him to improve.

It's the letter of Sunday, April 8th, that became a reality check for me. He discussed my aunt Betty, her husband Buddy, and their son Robert.

"I'm glad you got a chance to talk with Betty and I appreciate the fact that she does feel a little different and I'm sure if she does, that it is a result of prayer. I do hope that someday we will all be able to sit down and talk. I don't know though if Buddy or Robert will ever change. Buddy, I can, in a way, understand. But Robert really throws me as certainly nothing was forced on him and he was very much willing for anything to happen. Maybe though, someday, it will all work out."

This is not just an adult saying that a child was "willing." The adult was my father, and he was justifying his actions because my 13-year-old cousin was "willing."

As I read about sexual abuse, I find that it is not uncommon for a former victim to turn around and victimize another. I have to wonder if my father was molested at some point in his childhood to bring about this behavior. And by seeing nothing wrong, because my cousin was willing, he may have been reflecting on a time when he was in the same position and was willing himself. It's all just speculation, but I am trying to make sense of something that I will probably never understand.

The Child Molestation Research and Prevention Institute *(www. childmolestationprevention.org)* says child molestation is defined as the act of sexually touching a child, and a child is defined as one 13 years old or under. Male child molesters are predominately married, working, and very religious. They are often not at all who you think they would be, as evidenced by the case of my father and the men that molested me at our church. Friends and spouses often think that there must be some mistake, and continue to support the one accused. Also, when spouses hear an explanation, they usually believe their husband can change. Maybe they can. I hope my father did or at least suppressed the urges.

My parents blessed me with three names. My first name, James, was after my dad's father. My second name, Ronald, was after Ronald Berdeaux. At the time of my birth, Ronald was a 13-year-old Boy Scout in my dad's troop. In 1985, Ronald was arrested for the same charge as my father and Guy. He told me that he had been set up by his brother and nephew. With the current laws, this arrest placed him on the sexual offender's list. I do not know Ronald's circumstances, other than being gay and having the propensity to hire young men to work for him. However, it stands to reason that his going down this road might have been a result of being molested himself as a child. My third name is Monnie, after Monnie "Brownie" Flynn, another young Scout, 17 years old at the time of my birth, and part of the Flynn family that played an important role during this time, as evidenced in the letters.

After my father passed away, I would visit my two aunts *(His half-sisters)* who lived north of Tampa, Florida. Ronald Berdeaux, the former Scout after whom I was named, lived about an hour from them and I would also visit him. At the time, I had no idea of his involvement in this saga or that my aunt had been told by her mother, my dad's stepmother, that Ronald's mother had been the instigator from the beginning. Recently, after finding out about this part of my dad's life, I asked my aunt to tell me what she might know. She was surprised that I had not already known and that I was just now finding out. She said she had wondered why I would go visit Ronald knowing what his family had done. I still don't know for sure what their part in this chain of events might have been. But it's clear to me that they are a part of the story.

Before Ronald's mother passed away, she lived with him, and I would get a chance to visit with her. She would tell me stories of when she would babysit me, and how I loved to wear her high-heel shoes. In my dad's letter on Tuesday, April 10th, he wrote to my mother: "I know how you feel about Ron & the shoes. I'm just trying to think in my mind the best way to break him. I told you one thing that is working against us. He is with you and loves you so much that he wants to be like you. I think that if we can ever get to living together again so he can have a normal life, it will help. We will just have to find something to substitute for them and try that. It would be hard for him to understand if you just said no."

The Berdeauxes were only mentioned once in this set of letters. My dad was pleased my mother and I visited them, saying they still care about us. Although he added that they will probably never forgive him.

Again, forgive him for what? For what he was accused of by others, or for something a little more directly involved with their family? With Ronald gone, I contacted his twin brother, Donald. The twins would have been 16 at the time of my dad's arrest but Donald insisted he didn't remember anything. However, he encouraged me to get the court records. Could this be because he was sure that their family was not part of any legal documentation? Or that he already knew that the court records were no longer available?

Even without my mother's letters from this time period, it appears there was a bit more conflict. It was now mid-April, and the house still had not sold. It was on the market when my dad had gone to jail the previous November, so it had been at least six months, and because of that, keeping us in Miami and my dad in Charleston. My mother, along with working at the church and taking care of me, was making chicken pot pies for the Flynn's store and had agreed to make a dress for Kat Stone to earn a little extra cash.

My dad wrote, "One thing that you said in one of your letters sorta got off with me and I'm sure you didn't mean it just that way, but anyway, to set the record clear. I don't send you and Ron things to try and buy your love. I don't believe I am wrong when I feel that I have your love. I think that you have demonstrated that in many, many ways. I send you the little things that I send because I love you very much and enjoy so much thinking of you as I buy them. I'm pretty sure that with things having been like they are, I could never buy your love as I could never in this world place a value on what it has meant to have you love me. All that I ask is that you keep on loving me."

My father, in his letter from Sunday, April 15th, wrote: "You know, I have had a funny feeling all day today, ever since I got in from Sunday School today. I just believe the Lord wants me to do something and I'm not sure what it is, but somehow, I believe that I'll never be able to do it until I can get straightened out in Miami. In other words, until I can walk in Central Baptist or anywhere else in Miami. Sometimes I just get the feeling that I would like to come back to Miami and just go ahead and appear where I have usually appeared, and let the folks who want to do what talking they want to, and get it over with. I'm sure that after a while they will get tired of working on me and start on someone else. I have seen this happen before. I know this, that in the last six months, I haven't had but about three weeks total to spend with my family and I just don't think that I can continue this way. I just think of Ron growing up like he is and the few short years we will have with him, I just can't feel that this is right. I don't believe that the Lord let me escape imprisonment just to exist, and that is about all I'm doing now."

Ronald Berdeaux

THIRTEEN.

My mother and I made our only trip to Charleston on the weekend of April 21st. Not wanting us to travel alone, my dad had hoped that Brownie and Elaine would come with us. According to the letters, we stayed at the boarding house and the ladies there raved to my dad about us, saying he didn't exaggerate about his wife and child. He was so excited for us to come and looked forward to having the boarding house folks, as well as his new church friends, meet us. He had bragged about us for so long to all of them. My mother had baked cookies several times and mailed them to him. He had shared them with different people all the while singing praises about her cooking.

Again, tucked into one of his letters, are photos of my mother and me from that trip. And again, having been only three years old, I have no recollection of that weekend.

Finally, the house sold. The Church Education Director did come through. This left my mother with the chore of packing everything for the move. My dad, because of his job, was unable to come down and help.

It appears Guy had once again stirred something up. In a letter dated April 24th, my dad wrote: "I do hope that Brownie won't get mixed up in Guy's deal so that it would hurt his chances for a promotion. I'm really surprised that they are having the trial deal for Guy. I'm convinced he would have been smart to have let the matter drop. If you hear of him trying to get me in the deal, tell him he had better call and talk to me before he does anything as I might have a thing or two to say that might change his mind."

I don't know the connection between Brownie and Guy other than the Scouts. There had been no mention of Brownie being a part of the charges. And if he had, I don't think his parents, Mimi and D-Dad, would have been so close to our family then and through the years. Yet this mention intrigues me.

All of a sudden, plans changed. Independent Life was going to expand into Tennessee beginning with Chattanooga. In confidence, Cecil told my dad that he wanted him to go there and work with someone my dad knew well, who would be moving there to run the office. My dad talked with my mother, and it looked like it was going to happen. She was in the process of packing, and he was talking about coming down to Miami and leaving with her. I'm not sure if she had cold feet or what, but it became clear my mother wasn't ready to leave when he wanted to, so he told her to take her time and he'd go ahead and find a place so the furniture could be delivered there and not have to be stored. They talked about Mimi or Brownie Flynn driving up with us when we were ready to leave. It was a long trip and, again, he didn't want us to travel by ourselves.

As I read these letters, I was a bit confused, because of the story my mother told through the years of us coming to Tennessee and getting stopped for speeding. I never heard that one of our friends traveled with us. As I read through another letter or two, I began to put it all together. His letters are just his side of the story. Plus they talked often on the phone, so there were many things that could have been discussed then and not put in writing.

The letters never said, but I realized that the timing was off. My dad's last letter to her was dated Tuesday, May 8th, 1956. He told her that Chattanooga was 400 miles from Charleston, and that he would leave on Thursday, May 10, so he could arrive when we did. However, my thoughts went back to my grandfather, her father, and the April heart attack. On Wednesday, May 9th, the day we were to leave, my grandfather Broadway, passed away. I would have to think that our move got postponed. And the tears she was crying when the policeman pulled her over, as she crossed the Florida line, were for much more than just leaving home.

I think of how strong my mother must have been through all of this. I also think of how strong her mother was, as well. My grandmother had four daughters. The youngest, Bobbye, at 16 married and pregnant, had moved away. The next youngest, June, now divorced, had moved back home. The second to oldest, my mother Joyce, had all of Miami knowing her husband had been arrested for molesting young boy(s) from his Scout troop. And my grandmother's oldest daughter, Betty, was faced with her 13-year-old son being one of the boys molested, and her husband pressing charges and threatening to kill her brother-in-law. Then my grandfather suffered a heart attack, and a month later, at age 64, passed away as our family moved out of state. And, this grandmother was also the same woman who had hitchhiked from Michigan to Miami in 1920 in men's clothing with a girlfriend. So she had been strong all along.

My grandfather died on May 9th, the same date as my mother did 29 years apart. My father died on July 10th, as did his partner in crime, Guy Cutulo, 24 years apart. And the one rumored to be the start of the investigation, the one I'm named after, Ronald Berdeaux, died on July 25th. That was the same day, 11 years earlier, that my cousin Robert had committed suicide. I find it somehow disturbing, the way these dates are paired.

Another odd twist happened in 2014, when the Rev. Ernest Angley, the televangelist from that emotional 1985 final trip with my mother to the Atlanta market, was accused of many wrongdoings from former parishioners and staff, including inappropriate touching of his associate pastor and male members of Grace Cathedral.

Although there were many dead ends on this journey of discovery, I was able to find and speak with my late cousin Robert's fourth wife. She was married to him for 20 years, and still married to him when he chose to take his life. She was unaware of me and my family. Her mother-in-law, my aunt Betty, had only said that she had sisters, but that they didn't get along. She said that no one had ever mentioned to her anything regarding the molestation charges. She said that Robert had been troubled, was often depressed, and drunk heavily, but still, in his lowest times, never mentioned being molested by his uncle. It makes sense that they would be, but I can't know for sure if my father's actions were the cause of Robert's demons or not. However, she was very comforting, saying we are family and telling me not to believe everything I hear or read, because I will never know the whole truth. No one does. She encouraged me to focus on all of the good memories about my father, and suggested that I burn the letters.

My curiosity about Guy haunts me. I want to know what hold he had over my father, and whatever happened to him. In researching him, I found that he had married Addie in 1951. She was a widow, and 11 years older than he was, and they taught school together. Her tombstone reads, *"Teacher, Wife, Mother – None Better."* Her first husband died in 1943. I can't find a record of her divorcing Guy, but her tombstone has her maiden name and her first husband's last name. So at some point, she reverted back to her previous husband's name. And the assorted newspaper articles that listed my dad as married with a son, simply list Guy Cutulo. However, Addie is mentioned often in the "jailhouse" letters, so I assume that she did not separate from Guy until after his trials.

In going through the large box of family photos, there are numerous ones of young men. These are tiny school photos with names written on the back. Some, if not all, were Scouts. One name sounded familiar, and then it finally dawned on me that he was Guy's wife's son from her first marriage. The photo was a 1952 class picture and he was listed by his birth name. He would have been 13 at the time of their wedding. I can only imagine that, with the arrests, Addie chose to get her son away from him. In a Troop One annual banquet program from 1954, the boy was listed with the Cutulo last name. However, as I researched him, I found that not only had he excelled at Duke and had an amazing life, but he also had reverted back to his birth father's name. Unfortunately, he too had passed away before I could ask him about that brief time with Guy as his stepfather.

In 1943, Guy became an Eagle Scout in Bradenton, Florida. He would have been 26 years old at the time, leading me to believe that he was in some sort of leadership role, since he was too old to be a Scout. It is also my belief that my father and Guy met and became friends through a Scout function or competition.

Guy went into the Navy in 1944 and was stationed in the Philippines. Included in my box were two letters that Guy wrote in 1945 to my father. He tells of the sights, talks about missing his Scouts, and expresses concern for my dad's health. Because of heart issues, my dad was not able to serve his country.

The letters were raunchy as they described the natives. Plus he included lyrics to a song, which was nothing more than a series of dirty limericks. He talked about the native girls and what they would do for a pack of cigarettes, but that he wouldn't touch one "with a 10 ft. pole." However, he continued by saying, "I guess I'll have to be here a little while longer before I'll get the other."

The comment made earlier in one of my dad's Charleston letters from 1956, where he mentioned that Guy thought coming over to my dad's house was a "bad influence on him," didn't ring true when he continued his story in this 1945 letter from overseas. "All the stuff and time I missed in Miami, I got caught up with in San Francisco. They are hard to find but easy to keep and I was lucky, got a quick find and held it till I left. And to top it all off, 2 days before I left, a buddy of mine and myself ran into a queer and we got a free meal in a big hotel dining room and a trip to some swell night club. And when we were ready to go, we swiped $3.50 in change off the table and checked out when he was gone to the head. Boy, I know he must have been mad because we had told him we would go to his room that night. But the poor sucker forgot and turned his back and we haven't seen him since."

First, as with everything, I wonder why these letters were even saved. They show that at least ten years before the arrests, Guy felt comfortable enough to confide his sexual escapades with men to my father. Was my father that open minded? To me there is only one conclusion, which is that my father and Guy had been down this road before but to what extent, I don't know.

Guy's nephew was able to fill in a few blanks for me, and I was able to flesh his story out with a little more research. Before teaching school, Guy had worked for the American Red Cross and traveled quite a bit. Amazingly, I found a newspaper article from my very own city's daily newspaper, *The Tennessean*. It was dated August 24, 1947, five years before my birth, and nine years before we lived in Nashville. That was also the same year that Guy was listed in the graduating class of the University of Miami. The article talked about water safety training courses conducted by the American Red Cross at Dale Hollow reservoir. "The actual instruction was presented by Guy Cutulo, water safety instructor of the Red Cross."

Needless to say, Guy lost his teaching job once the arrests were made. One letter mentioned he delivered phonebooks and his nephew said he worked delivering cigars to small markets until the trials were over. At that point, he returned to the American Red Cross and eventually became their Director for Disaster Services for South Florida Area. The last article I find mentioning Guy was in the *Lakeland Ledger* on February 5, 1976. Guy was discussing the role and efforts that the United States would play regarding an earthquake in Guatemala.

Five months later, while vacationing in the Florida Keys, Guy suffered a heart attack and died on July 10th, the same day that my father would have his fatal accident, 24 years later.

Charleston, 1956

Guy Cutulo, Navy, 1945

Norris Broadway

FOURTEEN.

Nine months before my father found himself living on the 21st floor of the Dade County jail, and exactly two years to the day before he wrote his first letter from his Charleston self-imposed exile, the Troop One Annual Banquet was held at Central Baptist Church. Included in the February 5th, 1954 program was the Scoutmaster's Report. In it my father acknowledged the wonderful support of the committee men and assistant Scoutmasters in helping him to "mold the lives of fifty Boy Scouts." He thanked Central Baptist Church, along with Dr. Angell, for keeping the Scout program in the church budget.

He concluded with, *"For the privilege of working with these young men, I am grateful and it is my earnest prayer that I will never, in any way, betray the confidence and trust placed in me by sending me your sons." It is signed, "Respectfully, Robert L. York."*

The Boy Scouts of America have kept files on men they found unsuited to work with boys, similar to the Catholic church. These men had run into trouble or were turned in for inappropriate actions. They are known as the "Perversion Files" and go back as far as the 1920s. They came to light around 2010 as Scouts came forward with their claims of molestation. Thousands of names exist in these files.

However, for one reason or another, Robert York and Guy Cutulo of Troop One in Miami, Florida are not listed. It was a great relief when I couldn't find their names, and also a great sadness that I was having to look through this list. It was also a reality check when I saw names of men associated with troops in my area of Tennessee as recently as just a few years ago. In fact, as I am writing this, an article came out in our Nashville paper regarding an indictment of an ex-Scout leader for abusing five boys. What really hit me, although there is no connection to my story, was that his address was listed as on the same street, several blocks down, from my childhood home where I found the letters exposing the truth about my dad and the Boy Scouts.

TROOP ONE

ANNUAL BANQUET

CENTRAL BAPTIST CHURCH

February 5, 1954

Troop One Annual Banquet Program, 1954

I have a Central Baptist church bulletin from March, 1973 that announced a concert featuring the Belmont Chorale. I was a part of that touring choir as we made our way through the state of Florida singing at several Baptist churches. It was very special to me that one of those churches was our family church, Central Baptist, from when we lived in Miami. Often church members would offer lodging for the choir and I, along with my roommate John, stayed in the home of our family friends, Kat and Bud Stone. With my newfound knowledge of the events from the 1950s, I realize now that the Stones, as well as other church members, were painfully aware of my family's misfortune 20 years earlier. I have to think my parents would have been fearful someone might mention that to me. I feel confident that they asked the Stones, who stood by us through it all, to do their best to shield me from any repercussions that might have taken place during my visit making this just one more innocent memory that I now see in a different light.

Why am I sharing all of these secrets that have been buried for 60 years? I don't think that, now that I know them, I could hold this burden to myself. Reading these letters about our life, looking at the photos from that time, and the journey of opening one door that only leads to another and another has consumed me. And yet I know that I will never discover the whole story.

But, I am sure that I never knew the strength in my mother, or her mother, until this story unfolded. I never knew my dad as the conflicted, troubled man that he apparently was, or how he must have struggled to make amends.

I can only hope that the reader might find something positive in this story to take away with them. As one that was often sexually molested as a child, again not by my father or his friend, Guy, my wish would be that other victims be able to see through my eyes that you can carry on. It does not have to define you. Nor do you have to keep the cycle going.

I understand that as the reader, it will be easy for you to form an opinion about my parents. I can't sway you one way or another, nor would I want to. All I can do is present to you the facts as I know them. I may never be able to fill in the gaps. My father committed a crime over 60 years ago. He was arrested and pleaded

CENTRAL BAPTIST CHURCH
500 N.E. First Avenue
Miami, Florida 33132
Return Requested

The Messenger

Central Baptist Church
500 N.E. First Avenue
Miami, Florida 33132
CONRAD R. WILLARD TH.,D.
Pastor

Volume 45	March 2	Number 9

THE BELMONT BAPTIST COLLEGE CHORALE
of Nashville, Tennessee
will present
a Concert of Sacred & Secular Music
Monday Evening, March 5, 7:30 p.m.
Church Sanctuary and Dining Room

Supper served at 5:30 for the convenience of our church members. Price: $1.00.

Belmont Chorale, Miami, 1973

guilty. I do not know the effect on the families that came forward. Nor do I know if there were others that never spoke up. I'm sure there were temptations over the years and I pray that he resisted.

What I do know is that it left our family divided. True friends stood by us through the difficult time while others, according to the letters, chose to distance themselves. The end result found us leaving the city and state we called home. I personally am left with more questions than answers.

I have given you a glimpse into my life with the mother and father I knew. The letters are simply a time capsule of the eight weeks my father was in jail. I was not privy to their private conversations that took place each Sunday for two hours. I also have no idea of what was said between them when the first arrest was made or what they endured with the first trial. Nor do I know of their private conversations, outside of the letters, after he was released.

To me, the letters show a wife and mother growing stronger every day as she tried to keep her family together. I feel they show a husband and father accepting blame by pleading guilty, having his faith tested and, ultimately, bringing him closer to the Lord. A man who, I hope and believe, spent the next 44 years trying to make amends.

My mother's faith was strong enough to forgive him. I'm sure she felt that if the Lord could forgive him, then so could she. My dad was the outgoing, larger than life "face" of our family. She was the rock, the foundation, the example of how he needed to live his life. Her heart was big enough to love him in spite of his faults and his sins. I know now that she saved him, and I also know, for him, she was the love of his life. I have never doubted that they both loved me dearly, and maybe that is enough.

Dear Son -

Daddy misses his little boy.
You must be a sweet boy and
mind mommie. I know Santa
Clause will be good to you.
Daddy will be home soon
to see you. When you get
up Christmas morning you kiss
Mommie for Daddy.

You are a big boy and I
know mommie will have lots
of fun playing with you.

Kiss mommie for me. I
love you -

Love
Daddy

Acknowledgments

This book would not have been possible without the
help and guidance from
Trish Luna and Richard Courtney of
Open Book Nashville
www.openbooknashville.com
and the amazing
Mary Helen Clarke.

I also wish to thank
Alice Nicar, Barbara Carroll, William Fortner,
Mary Morrison, Frank Cutulo and Jim Harris
for their contribution to my story.

Cover concept and author photo by
Jade Reynolds

Cover image used under license from
Shutterstock.com

Please contact
National Resources for Sexual Assault Survivors and their Loved Ones
if you, or someone you know is in need of help.
www.rainn.org

CPSIA information can be obtained
at www.ICGtesting.com
Printed in the USA
LVOW08*0122070117
519756LV00002B/2/P